III

THE CENTRALIZATION OF ADMINISTRATION IN NEW YORK STATE

STUDIES IN HISTORY, ECONOMICS AND PUBLIC LAW

EDITED BY THE FACULTY OF POLITICAL SCIENCE OF
COLUMBIA UNIVERSITY
IN THE CITY OF NEW YORK

Volume IX]   [Number 3

THE CENTRALIZATION OF ADMINISTRATION

IN

NEW YORK STATE

BY

JOHN ARCHIBALD FAIRLIE

AMS PRESS
NEW YORK

98559

COLUMBIA UNIVERSITY
STUDIES IN THE
SOCIAL SCIENCES

25

The Series was formerly known as
Studies in History, Economics and Public Law.

Reprinted with the permission of Columbia University Press
From the edition of 1898, New York
First AMS EDITION published 1969
Manufactured in the United States of America

Library of Congress Catalogue Card Number: 77-77990

AMS PRESS, INC.
NEW YORK, N. Y. 10003

TABLE OF CONTENTS

CHAPTER I

CHAPTER II

PUBLIC EDUCATION

I. THE COMMON SCHOOL SYSTEM

CHAPTER III

CHARITIES AND CORRECTION

CHAPTER VI

Conclusion

CHAPTER I

INTRODUCTION

THE government first established over the early settlements within the present limits of New York State centralized all power in the hands of the Governor. The Directors General appointed by the Dutch West India Company and the first Governors sent over by the Duke of York possessed supreme legislative, judicial and executive powers; and these were exercised at first not merely in matters concerning the colony as a whole, but also over the purely local affairs of the various settlements.

The constitutional history of the colony during the seventeenth and eighteenth centuries is a history of constant aggressions upon the powers and prerogatives of the Governor. First, the outlying towns gained a practical independence in their local affairs, which was more fully recognized under the English rule by the Duke of York's Laws. Later, the cities of New York and Albany received a large degree of autonomy. The establishment of a legislature in 1691 was followed immediately by the creation of an elected county authority; and by gradual steps, during the next hundred years, the powers of both legislature and county supervisors were increased at the expense of the central executive.

This decentralization, however, did not become so complete in New York as it was in the New England States. Much that was done by the New England towns was in New

York performed by the county authorities; and a considerable part of the work of local administration remained subject to the control of the central government, through the power of appointing and removing sheriffs, justices of the peace and the mayors of the cities.[1] The maximum of decentralized administration was not reached until the third decade of the present century, when the local officers appointed by the central government became elective officials. The Common Councils of the cities were given the power to select their mayors by the Constitution of 1821, which also provided that the sheriffs should be elected in each county; and in 1826 a constitutional amendment made the justices of the peace elective. But even at this time central control over local officers was not altogether abandoned. The Constitution of 1821, while making the sheriffs elective, gave the Governor a limited power of removal over various county officers. Any sheriff, county clerk or register could be removed during his term of office, provided that before any removal, the officer should be given a copy of the charges against him, and an opportunity to be heard in his defense. These restrictions on the power of removal were serious limitations on the control which could be exercised over the local officers, but it is important to notice that even in the period when administration was most decentralized, there was at least a limited control over the county officials.

It was only a year after the adoption of the Constitution of 1821 that an important, though isolated, step was taken in the reflex movement toward a more centralized administration. This was the grant to the State Superintendent of Common Schools of an appellate jurisdiction over the acts

---

[1] Before the Revolution this appointing power was held by the Governor. By constitutional amendment in 1801 it was transferred to the Council of Appointment, consisting of four members of the State Senate elected annually by the Assembly.

of all local school officers. For the next three decades there was little further permanent advance in this direction; but since the middle of the century, and especially in the last twenty years, the return tide has become stronger, so that a considerable degree of centralization in New York State administration has now been reached.

In the first place, we may note the extensions of the central control first established: The Constitution of 1846 included the county coroners and district attorneys in the list of officers subject to removal by the Governor; and by a statute of 1892 county superintendents of the poor and notaries public are also included. Thus practically all the county administrative officers may be removed for proven violation of the law or other malfeasance in office. The authority of the State Superintendent of Schools has also been much extended from time to time; and that officer now possesses a most important power of control over the common school system throughout the State. Over the secondary schools and higher institutions of learning, a no less effective power of supervision is exercised by the Regents of the University.

In other spheres, formerly left to the independent action of local officials, there have been established central authorities with powers of investigation, advice, direction and sometimes of compulsion. In 1859 the State Board of Equalization was created; in 1867 the State Board of Charities, and in 1880 the State Board of Health. The Civil Service Commission through its power of approving the rules of City civil service boards has gained a slight control over the choice of subordinate officials in cities. The Comptroller has been given a limited control over the assessment and collection of the Inheritance Tax, and over county treas-

---

[1] *Laws of* 1892, c. 681.

urers; the supervision over the local assessment of the
general property tax has been made more stringent by the law
of 1896 establishing the Tax Commissioners; and a still more
thorough control has been established over the administration of the Liquor Tax Law, through the Excise Commissioner and his subordinates. The Commission of Prisons,
created in 1895, exercises a central supervision over county
jails and penitentiaries. Finally, by an Act of 1898, the
State Engineer is given important powers in preparing plans
and supervising the construction of certain highways, to
which State aid is to be given.

In some fields of governmental activity formerly left to
local governments a more complete centralization has been
established. The most important of these has been the
care of the insane, all of this class being now maintained in
the State insane hospitals. These and other charitable institutions, normal schools, State prisons and reformatories
provide a large sphere of direct State administration over
education, charities and correction, subjects which were, at
the beginning of the century, entirely under local control.

Direct State administration has also developed through
the creation of bureaus for the exercise of new governmental
functions. Thus the management of the State canals, the
supervision over certain kinds of business by the Superintendent of Banking, the Superintendent of Insurance and the
Railroad Commissioners, the work of factory inspection,
the arbitration of labor disputes, and a number of less important matters are completely centralized. The performance of some of these functions might have been entrusted
to the localities. A strict adherence to the policy of decentralized administration would have given over the supervision
of factories and the arbitration of labor disputes to local
officers. The direct administration of these functions by the
State is, therefore, significant and indicates that centralized

administration has been sometimes established in preference to a possible system of local administration. Even those bureaus which deal with matters which could not be attended to by local authorities have a part in the centralizing movement. They help to increase the total amount of direct State administration, and thus to make that relatively more important than the sphere of administration left to local officers.

The extent of this direct State administration deserves notice. There are over forty permanent State bureaus and commissions, besides a number of temporary boards appointed for special purposes. The roster of State employees occupies over 130 pages in the report of the Civil Service Commission and includes over 6,000 persons. These figures make it evident that the amount of central administration in New York State is very considerable. Its comparative importance may be indicated by noting that in 1890 the expenditures by State authorities (excluding funds turned over by the State to local officials) was almost equal to the expenditures by counties and towns.[1] Since 1890 the direct State expenditure of New York has nearly trebled, a large part of the increase being caused by the assumption of functions formerly left to the local governments. Apart from the cities, the expenditures of the local authorities are now insignificant compared with those of the State.

In addition to these tendencies toward State control and direct State administration, there has been a marked development of what may be called local centralization. This has taken place to some extent by the transfer of certain functions from the towns to the counties, notably the supervision of public schools and the administration of poor relief. But by far the most important phase of this development has

[1] Eleventh Census of the United States: *Wealth, Debt and Taxation*, ii., 441.

been in connection with the growth of cities and with recent changes in the organization of city government.

The progress of urban development acts of itself as a centralizing force in two directions. With the concentration of a large population, even within the original boundaries of a town, the local government becomes a mass of details, most of which require specialized knowledge and are of little general interest; popular knowledge of the government disappears, and the local officials, with a larger and growing field of action, are less and less subject to popular control. When, however, the increase of population goes beyond former boundaries, we have not only a steady increase of the influences mentioned, but in addition, as the boundaries of the city are extended, there is the abolition of former local governments and local centers of action. One city government takes the place of several towns or a large part of a county, and in the most recent and most noted instance several counties have been included within the limits of the single city of New York.

This process has been going on throughout the United States, but in New York State it has reached vast and most significant dimensions. In 1790 New York city was the only community in the State of more than 8,000 population, and its population was less than one-tenth of the entire State. By 1830 there were seven cities of over 8,000, and the urban population had increased in the forty years nine-fold; but the relative increase of city population had not as yet become marked—the ratio in 1830 was only fourteen per cent. It is since 1830 that the wave of urban movement has set in most strongly. In the next forty years the city population had again been multiplied by nine, and had reached forty-three per cent. of the entire population of the State. By 1890, the city population was double that of 1870, and the thirty-six cities of over 8,000 inhabitants had nearly sixty per cent. of the population of the State.[1] During these six decades the non-urban population of the State has remained at almost the same figures. Since 1890 the increase of city population has continued with no signs of cessation. By the extension of the boundaries of New York City one-half of the inhabitants of the State came under one local government, and almost a half of the rest are in the other forty cities of the State. Hardly a fourth of the people of New York State are in communities small enough to retain effective local self-government, and deducting the inhabitants of incorporated villages, probably less than fifteen per cent. are under the true democracy of the town meeting.

The centralization in local government resulting from the development of urban communities has been further intensified by changes in the organization of city governments. The first changes from the colonial system of council government had tended to a distribution of functions among independent executive boards; but the recent tendency has been to concentrate authority in the hands of the Mayor, through his power of appointment and removal of the heads of departments, and by requiring a large majority to override his vetoes.

The first city charter to adopt this centralizing principle

[1] URBAN POPULATION OF NEW YORK STATE.

	1790.	1810.	1830.	1850.	1870.	1890.
New York City.......	33,131	96,373	197,112	515,547	942,292	1,515,301
Brooklyn	......	......	....	96,838	396,099	806,343
Other cities over 8,000.	......	10,762	74,369	236,000	540,000	1,172,000
Total urban population	33,131	107,135	271,481	848,000	1,890,000	3,494,000
Population of the State	340,120	959,049	1,918,608	3,097,394	4,382,759	5,997,853
Per cent. of urban population	10%	11%	14%	27%	43%	58%
Number of cities with over 8,000 population	1	2	7	14	23	36

was the revised charter for Brooklyn of 1882, which gave the Mayor of that city absolute power of appointing nearly all the heads of the city departments. In 1884 the Mayor of New York City was given absolute power of appointment by taking away the confirmatory power of the Board of Aldermen; but removals were subject to the consent of the Governor until 1895, when an absolute power of removal was granted for the first six months of each Mayor's term. By 1891, the Mayor's absolute power of appointment of most or all of the department heads had been established in Long Island City, Ithaca, Syracuse and Utica. In Binghamton, Newburgh, Poughkeepsie and Yonkers the Mayor held the independent power of appointing some officials, although for most positions the confirmation of the Council was necessary.[1] In 1891 a revision of the Buffalo charter established the Mayor's independent appointing power in that city;[2] and charter revisions for Hudson in 1895 and Kingston in 1896, included these also in the list of cities having autocratic Mayors.[3] On the other hand, Troy and Yonkers have had complete charter revisions without introducing this principle,[4] and only two of the ten cities incorporated since 1890 give the Mayor this absolute control over appointments.[5]

The charter for New York city,[6] however, introduces a still further centralization in the hands of the Mayor. His absolute power of removal is still limited to the first six months of his term; but his control over the expenditures is so complete that his power over the entire administration is much increased. This control over the finances is secured first, by the fact that he and his appointees constitute a

[1] *Fassett Committee Report.*   [2] *Laws of* 1891, c. 105.

[3] *Ibid.,* 1895, c. 751. *Laws of* 1896, c. 747.   [4] *Ibid.,* 1895, c. 277; c. 635.

[5] Geneva and North Tonawanda. *Laws of* 1897, c. 360; c. 361.

[6] *Laws of* 1897, c. 378.

majority of the board of estimate and apportionment which frames the budget for all the city departments; and secondly, by his veto over any change in the budget made by the Council, which veto can only be overridden by a five-sixths vote of all the members of both branches of the Council. The views of the Mayor will thus, in practice, determine the expenditure of every department of the city government; and through this financial control he can limit, if he cannot altogether direct, the work of the departments, even after his power of removal has expired. The centralization is made even more complete by the fact that these administrative departments now possess most of the authority formerly possessed by the City Council. Another change made by the new charter has been the extension of the Mayor's term to four years, so that for this length of time the government of the city of New York is almost completely in the control of one man.

The uniform charter for the government of cities of the second class,[1] which goes into effect on January 1st, 1900, places a much more sweeping power of control in the hands of the Mayors of these cities. All of the administrative officers, except the Comptroller, Treasurer and Assessors are to be appointed by the Mayor, and to be subject to his absolute power of removal at any time during their term of office. Moreover, a meeting of these heads of the departments with the Mayor for consultation and advice is to be held at least once a month, while the Mayor can at any time call for reports or summon conferences. It is thus the evident purpose of the law that the Mayor shall direct and control the administration in every way. If further authority were needed, it could be secured by the Mayor's control over the board of estimate, and over the board of contract

[1] Rochester, Syracuse, Albany and Troy.

and supply, which makes all contracts where the cost exceeds two hundred dollars. He and his appointees constitute a majority of the former board, and four of the five members on the latter. Finally, the Mayor may veto any ordinance or any part of an ordinance passed by the common council; and his veto can be overcome only by a three-fourths vote of the entire council.

It is the purpose of this essay to consider, in some detail, those of the centralizing tendencies here outlined where a State administrative control or direct State administration has been established in matters formerly left to the independent action of the localities. In these departments centralization indicates a more open departure from the former policy of local independence than in the other instances mentioned. At the same time it is possible in these fields of governmental action to trace the steps in the centralizing movement, to measure the stage now reached, and by a comparison of present with earlier conditions to consider whether or not the results have justified the change of policy.

The field of education, in which central control first appeared and in which it has been farthest developed, will be given first consideration. The central authorities in the two departments of common schools and higher education have been so completely differentiated that a separate treatment must be given of each; but the fact that both authorities deal with the same general subject of education justifies uniting them in the one chapter. The second chapter—on Charities and Correction—deals with three State authorities. The grouping of the State Commission in Lunacy and the State Board of Charities is warranted by the historical development as well as by the kindred nature of the subjects; and the work of the Commission of Prisons is sufficiently allied to include it in the same division. The relations of the State Board of Health to the local authorities have no close connection with other subjects, and fall naturally into a separate chapter. Following this, in the chapter on Taxation and Local Finance, three different authorities are included—the State Tax Commissioners, the State Comptroller and the Excise Commissioner.

After the consideration of the development, present status and results of the leading centralizing tendencies, an attempt will be made in the concluding chapter to analyze the general causes of the movement and to discuss the principles which should determine administrative policy.

CHAPTER II

PUBLIC EDUCATION

I. THE COMMON SCHOOL SYSTEM

1. *The Development of State Aid and State Control*

THE early history of education in New York gives little promise of the high degree of central control which has come to be established during the present century. Throughout the colonial period the only action by the Province legislature concerned the establishment of academies, and whatever was done in the way of common school education was through private or local action.[1] The relations of the State government to this latter problem begin with the law of 1795,[2] appropriating £20,000 annually for the encouragement of schools. This amount the legislature apportioned among the different counties; the apportionment to the various towns was entrusted to the supervisors in each county, and the local management was entirely in the hands of elected town commissioners and school district trustees. The trustees were required to make reports to the town commissioners as the basis for the district apportionment of the State appropriation; and reports of the number of schools, scholars and days of instruction were to be forwarded through the town commissioners and county treas-

---

[1] As early as 1691 a bill was proposed in the New York Assembly "to appoint a school-master for the educating and instructing of children and youth, to read and write English in every Town in the Province." No action was taken on this bill.—*Journal of New York Assembly*, 1691–1743, p. 7.

[2] *Laws of* 1795, c. 75.

22

urers to the Secretary's office at Albany. There is, however, no provision for either State or county control or supervision in the system of school administration thus set up; and although the State appropriation was continued annually for ten years, there was no action taken towards inspection or control of the schools aided from the State funds.

In 1805 the school appropriation was allowed to lapse, and although the accumulation of a Common School Fund was at the same time provided for, there was to be no distribution until the annual interest of this fund amounted to $50,000. It was not until 1814 that this situation was reached, and during this interval common school education became again entirely a subject for local action or inaction as the case might be. With the renewal of State aid for schools from the interest of the Common School Fund, Acts were passed for the organization of the school system throughout the State.[1] The Massachusetts "district system" was made the basis, probably because existing local schools were established on that plan. Each district meeting of freeholders and taxpayers was authorized to locate its school, levy local taxes, and elect a board of trustees, who employed the teachers and directed the management of the schools. There were also to be school commissioners in each town, to whom the trustees were to make reports, and town inspectors to examine candidates for positions as teachers.

The grants from the State were made conditional on the raising of an equal amount by local taxation, and the first step was taken in the direction of central supervision by providing for a Superintendent of Common Schools, selected by the Council of Appointment, at an annual salary of $400. The chief duties of this officer were in the management of

[1] *Laws of* 1812, c. 242. *Laws of* 1814, c. 192.

the Common School Fund, his powers of control over the schools and local officers being but slight. He was, however, to prepare plans for the better organization of the schools, to apportion the State appropriation among the counties according to their population, and the reports of the school trustees to the town commissioners were to be forwarded to him.

In the introduction and organization of the new school system, the first Superintendent, Gideon Hawley, did not limit himself to the duties specified in the statute. By his activity he demonstrated the possibilities of his position, and the successful establishment within eight years of 5,500 schools with an enrollment of over 300,000 pupils has been ascribed in very large degree to his work. The uncalled for removal of Superintendent Hawley, in 1821, caused the legislature, as a means of censuring this action of the Council of Appointment, to transfer the duties of Superintendent of Schools to the Secretary of State. This change was in effect a reduction of the central control over the educational system, for although that officer could perform the specific duties laid down in the law, his other functions made impossible the same active work outside the letter of the statute as could be done by a separate official.

The first step in the direction of an increase in the central control was in 1822,[1] when the acting Superintendent of Schools was given an appellate and final jurisdiction over all acts and decisions of local school officials. The power thus conferred on the State Superintendent has been of the greatest importance; it in effect constituted him an administrative court, and his decisions on the thousands of cases that have been presented form a body of administrative law controlling the powers and duties of all local school of-

---

[1] *Laws of* 1822, c. 245.

ficials. The scope and significance of this authority will be considered in detail later; it is only necessary here to note its general character and its place in the historical development of central control.

The need for a more effective supervision of the schools and local school authorities soon began to be felt. Governor De Witt Clinton, in his message to the Legislature in 1826, pointed out that the Superintendent of Schools was prevented by his other official duties as Secretary of State from visiting the schools in person, while in fact he had no legal authority to make such visits. The Governor held that "a visitorial authority for the purpose of detecting abuses in the application of the funds, of examining into the modes and plans of instruction, and of suggesting improvements would unquestionably be attended with the most propitious effects."[1] These opinions were endorsed by the Literature Committee of the State Senate, whose chairman urged that "the State, which contributes so large a proportion of the compensation of the teachers, has a right to direct its application in such a way as to effect the object of procuring useful instruction."[2] Similar recommendations were made in the following year by the Secretary of State in his capacity as Superintendent of Schools. But no action was taken by the legislature; and the local authorities continued for fifteen years more to direct the management of the schools free from any effective inspection and supervision.

In 1839, John C. Spencer, Chairman of the Senate Literature Committee of 1826, became Secretary of State, and *ex-officio* Superintendent of Common Schools. With the earlier proposals still in mind, he secured from the legislature the authority to appoint unsalaried county boards of visitors to

[1] S. S. Randall: *History of the Common School System of the State of New York*, p. 51.

[2] Randall, *op. cit.*, 101, 105.

visit the schools and report with suggestions for improvement.[1] The reports of these boards of visitors recommended the establishment of an efficient and systematic county supervision under the general direction of the State bureau, as a substitute for the existing inefficient method of town inspection. These reports and the greater official influence now held by Mr. Spencer secured the enactment, in 1841, of the scheme proposed by him fifteen years before.

The Act of 1841[2] provided for the appointment by the Secretary of State of a Deputy Superintendent of Schools, thus making possible a greater central activity in carrying out the powers conferred by previous statutes. For the visitation and inspection of the schools, there was to be a Superintendent in each county, who should recommend to school trustees and teachers the proper studies, books, discipline and conduct of the schools; examine and grant certificates of qualification to teachers; and also decide in the first instance on appeals subject to the jurisdiction of the State Superintendent. These county superintendents, although appointed by the supervisors in each county, were to act subject to the rules and regulations of the Superintendent of Schools, and half of their salaries was paid by the State. With the Deputy Superintendent at Albany and this corps of county officials, a much more thorough system of school supervision and a much more effective central control was made possible.

The new system of inspection brought about great improvements in school administration, and its benefits were so clear that Superintendent of Schools Young, who when he succeeded Mr. Spencer as Secretary of State was a violent opponent of the change, soon became its enthusiastic supporter.[3] Legislative committees and prominent educators

---

[1] *Laws of* 1839, c. 330.   [2] *Ibid.,* 1841, c. 260.

[3] *Reports of Supt. of Schools,* 1843, 1844, 1845.

also strongly approved of the plan and methods adopted. Nevertheless, there arose a strong demand for the abolition of this system of supervision.[1] Local trustees and town commissioners were not pleased to find their former independence interfered with, while injudicious political selections by supervisors in some counties resulted in the appointment of some incapable and oppressive officials,[2] For these and other reasons the clamor against the Act continued, the pressure on the legislature finally became too strong, and in 1847 the county superintendent system was abolished.[3] On the face of it, the result was to place the town and district officers in direct connection with the State department; but in fact, as the State Superintendents recognized, any effective supervision of the local officers without a corps of officers acting under the direction of the State bureau was impossible, and the result was plainly a long step in the direction of decentralization.

The reaction was only temporary. Other forces were at work, and soon new measures were taken which so increased the amount of State aid to the common schools that a return to the policy of further State intervention in the management of the schools was inevitable. Already in 1838 the interest of the United States Deposit Fund had been appropriated to the schools,[4] increasing the annual State appropriation from $110,000 to $275,000. Just at the time the office of county superintendent was abolished the agitation for free schools was beginning; in 1849 the Free School Act was adopted by a referendum vote;[5] and, although the practical realization of free schools did not come until much later, an important step in that direction was taken in 1851, when a State tax of $800,000 was imposed by the legislature for the support of the common schools, in addition to the

[1] Randall: *op. cit.*, 177.   [2] *Ibid.*, 233.
[3] *Laws of* 1847, c. 480.   [4] *Ibid.*, 1838, c. 237.   [5] *Ibid.*, 1849, c. 151.

income of the Common School and United States Deposit Funds.

The increase of State aid was not for the purpose of increasing State control, for the new appropriation was turned over to the town commissioners and district trustees, to be expended at their discretion in the same way as the earlier grants. Nevertheless, the increased State appropriation paved the way for a larger degree of inspection and supervision of the schools, and in fact made a more thorough control almost essential.

An important step in this direction was the organization, in 1854, of a separate Department of Public Instruction.[1] The general oversight of the schools had hitherto been entrusted to an official burdened with many other duties, and although since 1841 there had been a special Deputy Superintendent of Public Instruction, his duties were those of a subordinate, and the Secretary of State remained as the head of the school system. An independent Superintendent of Public Instruction, freed from all other functions, could necessarily exercise a greater activity beyond the sphere of statutory duties. In addition to the former powers of the Secretary of State, the Superintendent of Public Instruction was given authority to visit the schools and make inquiries into the course of instruction, management and discipline. Even although he could not personally visit any large number of schools, the grant of this power is significant of the tendency towards a larger control over the local school officers.

In 1856 the State school tax was changed from a tax for a fixed sum to a ¾ mill tax,[2] which at the existing valuation gave an immediate increase of $300,000 in the State grants for schools. At the same time came the re-establishment of

---

[1] *Laws of* 1854, c. 97.   [2] *Ibid.*, 1856, c. 179.

an effective system of supervision, which had been urged constantly by the State Superintendents since the repeal of the county superintendent system in 1847. The new system differed in some respects from that established in 1841. There was to be a school commissioner for each Assembly District, instead of a Superintendent for each county, and the commissioners were to be elected instead of appointed by the board of supervisors. Although chosen by local election, the district commissioners being subject to the rules and regulations of the State Superintendent, and receiving their salary from State funds on his order, were under the direction of that officer, and the introduction of the system marks an important step in the extension of state control. The powers and duties of the district commissioners included the examination of the management, instruction and discipline of the schools, and the condition of school buildings and grounds; the recommendation of improvements in all these lines; the examination, licensing and annulling licenses of teachers, and the organization of teachers' institutes. The authority of the district commissioners did not, however, include the city schools.

The re-introduction of the system of supervision evoked at first considerable complaint,[1] but the State Superintendents were satisfied that it produced good results, and it has continued as a permanent part of the New York school system. Acting State Superintendent Keyes, in his report for 1862, summarizes the benefits derived from the system in these words: "An officer of extended jurisdiction has a higher and wider range of influence, is more generally consulted upon questions of school policy and in matters of school controversy, and his opinions and advice have a consequence and weight that cannot attach to a local officer of limited jurisdiction."[2]

[1] Randall, *op. cit.*, 338.   [2] *Ibid.*, 349.

After the establishment of the commissioner system of supervision, the next few years showed no new developments in the New York school system. But in the middle of the decade, 1860–1870, came a new period of activity, in which the scope of both local and central governmental action along educational lines was much increased. The general revision of the School Law in 1864[1] contains some additions to the powers of the State Superintendent over the schools, authorizing him to appoint unsalaried school visitors in the counties, and to remove school commissioners or other school officers for wilful violation or neglect of duty. The powers of the district commissioners were also increased by giving them authority to condemn unfit school buildings, and to direct trustees to make necessary repairs, in addition to their former powers of recommendation. The most important advance at this time was in the introduction of central control in the management of teachers' institutes. The Act of 1856 had authorized the district commissioners to organize such institutes in the various counties; and in 1861 they were held in 47 counties, with an attendance of 7,488 teachers. Under the law of 1864, the organization of such an institute in every county was required, a State appropriation was set aside for their support, and they were placed more directly under the jurisdiction of the State Superintendent by requiring the district commissioners to act in arranging these meetings under his˜advice and direction, and further by authorizing him to employ persons to conduct and teach at the institutes. These gatherings of the teachers for even a single week in each year gave opportunity for helpful comparisons of methods, and increased the interest and enthusiasm of those attending for their work. The extension of the State Superintendent's authority over this

---

[1] *Laws*, 1864, c. 555.

field was, therefore, an important advance in his control of the educational system, and enabled him to influence more directly than before the instruction given in the district schools.

In addition to the institutes intended for those actually engaged in teaching, a system of normal schools for training a body of teachers was also developed. The State Normal School at Albany was established in 1844;[1] in 1866 the more important State officers were constituted a Commission to determine the location of other schools,[2] and within four years eight additional normal schools had been established in different parts of the State. The administration of this normal school system was entirely centralized under the control of the State Superintendent. For each school there was provided a local board to direct and supervise the instruction; but these boards were appointed by the State Superintendent, and all their more important acts were subject to his approval.

Along with these developments of central control over school administration there went a rapid increase in the amount of State aid. In 1863, the State School Tax amounted to a little over $1,000,000; in 1868, it was $2,400,-000. At the same time came the final step in the complete realization of the Free School Act of 1849; in 1867 an Act was passed by the Legislature abolishing all rate bills in the public schools, making them free to every scholar. The increased State activity in educational affairs was accompanied by a no less increase in local educational activity in the same period. This is shown clearly by the enormous increase of yearly local taxation for school purposes from $2,500,000 in 1863 to $7,000,000 in 1869; and it is worthy of note that this development is equally striking in both city and rural taxation.

[1] *Laws of* 1844, c. 311.　　　[2] *Ibid.*, 1866, c. 466.

The unusual progress shown during these few years both in administrative centralization and in the extension of school facilities and equipment was followed by a long period in which little further advance was made. For nearly twenty years there was no extension of the powers of the State authorities, and during these years the increase in both State and local expenditure for schools was at a rate which barely kept pace with the growth of population. In the last twelve years, however, there have been further rapid advances along both lines. From 1885 to 1896 the annual State school tax increased from $3,000,000 to $4,000,000; the total annual expenditure for school purposes rose from less than $12,000,000 to $25,000,000; and at the same time there has been a considerable development of central control over the school system.

Thus, in 1887, a uniform system of teachers' examinations under the direction of the State Department was substituted for the former method of independent commissioner examinations. In 1889, the supervision of teachers' training classes in high schools and academies was transferred from the Regents of the State University to the Superintendent of Public Instruction. The Compulsory Education Law of 1894 provided for a small force of inspectors attached to the State department to investigate the enforcement of the Law. These and other minor additions to the authority of the State Superintendent in the aggregate materially strengthen the central control over the school system.

To review this brief sketch:—we note that the development toward central control in the first half of the century was not without reactionary steps. The office of State Superintendent of Schools, created in 1812, was abolished in 1821, and the powers of that officer conferred on another official busied with other and unrelated duties. The county superintendent system of supervision, established in 1841, was

abandoned after six years' experience. Nevertheless, even
in this period, there were permanent measures in the direction of increasing the central authority, prominent among
these being the appellate jurisdiction of the State Superintendent, conferred in 1822, and the provision for a Deputy
Superintendent in 1841. Since the creation of a separate
Department of Public Instruction in 1854, the movement
has been uniformly but not always steadily in the direction
of strengthening the authority of that department. The
system of district commissioners, established in 1856, made
possible a closer supervision of the local schools; in the legislation of 1864–67 the State Superintendent's control was
increased through the supervision of training teachers, and
in other details; during the last ten years the entire system
of examining teachers has been placed under his immediate direction, and the supervision of school attendance and
other details of school management have come to a greater
or less degree under his general oversight. The present
stage of central control has been reached not by any sudden
change of policy, but through a series of measures extending over a period of a hundred years.

This development of central control has moreover been
closely connected with the increase of State grants. For although State aid does not seem to have been given for the
purpose of establishing control, the State appropriations
have rendered necessary State supervision, and, as these
State grants have increased, the control over the local
authorities has been made more complete and more effective.

2. *Local School Authorities*

The discussion of the existing system of State control over
the public school system necessitates some understanding of
the local organizations over which this control is exercised.
It is not possible to give here any detailed account of the

various local authorities and their functions in school administration; but with a brief statement of the broader outlines of this organization the fuller discussion of the authority of the State Superintendent of Public Instruction will be more intelligible, and his position in the general school system better understood.

The School District.—The primary unit for rural school administration in New York is still the school district. There are now over 11,000 such districts in the State, an average of twelve to each town. In each district there is a meeting of all tax-payers and resident citizens on the last Tuesday in August of each year for the discussion and decision of school matters for the district. This district meeting, which is in fact a town meeting on a small scale, appoints its chairman, elects district officers (one or three trustees, a district clerk, collector and librarian), designates schoolhouse sites, selects text-books, and votes local taxes for school purposes to supplement the district's share of the state grant. The taxing power of the district meeting is however limited to certain specified purposes, for certain of which a maximum amount is also set in the statute; while the trustees are also authorized to levy a tax to pay deficiencies in the teacher's salary, even if no vote is passed by the district meeting.

The important officer of a school district is the trustee. If a district has a sole trustee, his term is one year; if there are three trustees, one is chosen each year for a three years' term. The trustees of every school district prepare the tax list and direct the collection of the school tax in their district. They carry out the votes of the district meeting in regard to the purchase or lease of a school-house site, and the erection, purchase or lease of a school house. They have also the custody of the school house, which they must keep in repair, suitably furnished and supplied with fuel;

they must engage a teacher under contract, and in order to
secure the quota of State aid the school must be in operation for at least 32 weeks in the year. For expenses incurred under these provisions the trustees can levy a tax,
even without special authorization from the district meeting.

Without dwelling on the various arguments for and against
the district system, we need only notice here some of the
actual results of the system in this State. In 1870 there
were 1,500 school districts with an average daily attendance
of less than ten; to-day there are more than 3,000 such districts, and over 7,500 of the 11,000 rural districts with an
average attendance of less than twenty. There are 2,750
districts in the State where the total resident population of
school age is less than twenty, and 500 districts where it is
less than ten.[1] In one district a teacher was appointed who
received the district's share of the State appropriation and
conducted school for three weeks with no pupils in attendance, as the only two children in the district had been kept
at home by illness. These small districts are obviously unable to take advantage of the vast improvements in educational methods, and with the retention of the district system
the inefficiency of rural schools must be expected to become more and more marked. Every State Superintendent since 1860 has approved of the abolition of the district
system, and the adoption in its stead of the township system; but in the face of their opinion, the judgment of other
experienced educators, and the example of twenty-three
States, the petty school district is still retained in the rural
sections of New York State.

Union Free School Districts. The only legislation looking
toward the disappearance of the "district system" in this
State has been the statute of 1853 permitting the consolida-

---

[1] *Report of Superintendent of Public Instruction*, xlii, 9; xliii, 10.

tion of two or more districts into a Union Free School District, on the vote of the inhabitants at a meeting held for the purpose. A single school district may in the same manner be established as a Union Free School District.

In each such Union Free School District there is a board of education, consisting of nine unpaid trustees, three elected each year for a term of three years. These boards of education have much the same authority as the trustees of a district school, and in some matters have also the powers of a district meeting. They have charge and possession of all the school property. They employ teachers, establish rules on school discipline, prescribe text-books, grade and classify the course of study, and have in all respects the superintendence, management and control of the schools in the union districts. The boards of education are in addition made bodies corporate, and in union districts whose limits do not correspond with those of an incorporated city or village they have power to appoint a district treasurer and collector, and to call special meetings of the voters of the union district. If any annual union district meeting does not vote a tax to cover the estimates of school expenses, the board of education may levy the tax without such vote.

The School Commissioners. In the ascending scale of school administrative officials in New York, the second rank is held by the school commissioners. The State, outside of the cities, is divided into 114 commissioner districts, 14 of which include an entire county, while the remaining counties are each divided into two or three districts. The smallest commissioner district has 13 school districts, the largest has 179, but generally the number is not far from 100. Where there are more than 200 school districts under one commissioner, the supervisors of the county are authorized to divide the commissioner district. The school commissioners are elected by the voters of the district, at the general

State elections, for a term of three years, women being eligible
and sometimes chosen.   The salary is $1,000 a year from
the State, to which the board of supervisors must add, from
the county revenues, $200 for expenses; they may also make
any increase in the salary they may deem advisable.

The school commissioners are required: (1) to visit
and inspect all the schools in their respective districts at
least once a year; (2) to consult with and advise the trustees
in all matters relating to the studies, discipline and management of the schools; and (3) to order repairs to school-
houses, the abatement of nuisances, and the construction of
new school buildings where necessary.   They also license
five-sixths of the entire teaching force of the State; they have
the power to alter school district boundaries, and to form
new districts; and sites for school-houses must have their
approval.   The responsibility and authority of the school
commissioners over the management and improvement of
the schools are thus extensive, and their duties are such as to
call for considerable ability and marked educational requirements.   A qualified and earnest commissioner has ample
opportunities to secure more competent teachers and better
school accommodations within his district, and the educational interests of a large part of the State depend on the
faithful discharge of their duties by these officers.

The testimony of the State Superintendents indicates that
the great body of commissioners are conscientious and competent officials, and it is encouraging to note that in the last
election, of the 114 commissioners, 60 were re-elected, and
14 others had previous experience in this work.[1]   There are,
however, a good number of commissioners chosen who lack
the necessary qualifications.   Complaints are made that
political influence and log-rolling between the political can-

---

[1] *Report of Superintendent of Public Instruction*, xliii, 12.   In 1890, 51 Commissioners were re-elected.

didates often result in the election of inefficient and incompetent persons, and that there have been some commissioners who could not pass the higher examinations for the teachers whose work they are supposed to criticise.[1] The establishment of educational qualifications for the office has been proposed, and also a change in the method of selection from a popular election to appointment by the County Judges.[2]

Cities and Incorporated Villages. In all the cities, and in a considerable number of the incorporated villages of the State, the local school management is regulated by special statutes, and in consequence there are wide variations in the methods and organization. In general, however, there is a board of education, though the number of its members and the method of selecting them are differently regulated for each city or village. These city boards of education act much as the boards of education in the union free school districts, but having usually a number of schools under their control, there is also a Superintendent of Schools (who in the larger cities has also assistants) for the detailed inspection and direction of the schools.

All but four of the cities are excepted from the commissioner districts, so that the city superintendents and boards of education are not within the jurisdiction of any school commissioner. Over the four excepted cities and thirty villages with superintendents, the school commissioners have the same legal powers as in the rural districts; but, naturally, with the better organization in these more urban districts, there is less occasion for the exercise of their authority.

Although the city boards of education are not within the jurisdiction of the school commissioners, they are not merged into the city corporations so as to lose their charac-

[1] *Report of Superintendent of Public Instruction*, xxiii, 23; xxxvi, 20; xlii, 8.
[2] *Ibid.*, xxxvi, 29; xli, 28; xliii, 13.

ter as agents of the State and part of the general school system. This point has been specifically decided by the
Supreme Court, which holds that a city board of education
is not a part of the city corporation, "but is itself a local
school corporation, like every board of school district trustees throughout the State, and is like every such board an
integral part of the general school system of the State. It
is a State and not a city agency, doing State and not city
work and functions."[1]

3. *The State Superintendent of Public Instruction*

At the head of the New York common school system is
the State Superintendent of Public Instruction, elected by
joint ballot of both houses of the legislature for a term of
three years, at a salary of $5,000 a year. His department
is one of the most important of the State administrative
bureaus, and is the most striking illustration in New York
State of a high degree of central administrative control exercised over local officials. This control over the instruction
and management of the common schools is exercised in
several ways, each of which requires separate consideration.

In the apportionment of the State tax to the various
school districts, the State Superintendent, though closely

---

[1] Ridemour *vs.* Board of Education of Brooklyn. *N. Y. State Reporter*, vol.
72, p. 155.

The same point is established by two legislative decisions allowing an inspector
of schools of New York (1876) and a member of the board of education of Albany (1880) to hold seats in the State legislature, although the charters of these
cities declared the board of education to be a department of the city government
and enumerated the members of the board in the list of city officers, and the
State Constitution provided that no officer under any city government should be
eligible to the legislature. The decisions of the investigating committees, which
in both cases were adopted by the house concerned without a dissenting vote,
were that no matter what was said in the charters "the board of education was
possessed of powers and charged with the performance of duties not of a corporate or local character, but for the maintenance of a State system of education."—
A. S. Draper in *Educational Review*, xv., 111.

bound by the provisions of the statute, is given a limited degree of discretionary authority. In making the allotments, he must be satisfied that each school district maintains school for at least 160 school days in each year, and that each city, village or union free school district with over 5,000 population employs a competent person as Superintendent, whose time is exclusively devoted to the general supervision of the public schools. Further, the State Superintendent may withhold a district's share for wilful disobedience to any of his decisions, orders or regulations, and he may withhold one-half of the allotment from any city or district which in his judgment wilfully omits to enforce the Truant Law.

In the second place, the State Superintendent is authorized to prepare the forms and regulations for the reports which the local school officers make to him, and to transmit them to the local officers "with such information and instructions as he shall deem conducive to the proper organization of the common schools, and the due execution of their duties by the school officers." He has also authority to remove school officers for violation or neglect of such orders, so that he can compel the local officers to give the information as to the condition of their schools.

Further, the whole body of school commissioners may be considered as subordinates of the State Superintendent. His authority over them is limited by the fact that he does not have any control in their selection; but in the discharge of their many functions they are required to act under rules and regulations adopted by the State Superintendent, and the authority to remove school commissioners for wilful violation or neglect of duty places in his hands the means to secure obedience to the law and to his instructions. The actual exercise of these compulsory powers is infrequent, since the possession of the power is usually sufficient to secure obedience.

The appellate jurisdiction of the State Superintendent gives him a comprehensive authority over the whole field of school management; and is of such importance both in powers granted and in the actual exercise of these powers as to deserve fuller consideration. The right of appeal to the State Superintendent may be exercised by:

"Any person conceiving himself aggrieved in consequence of any decision made:

" 1. By a school district meeting."

" 2. By any school commissioner or school commissioners and other officers in forming or altering, or refusing to form or alter any school district, or in refusing to apportion any school moneys to any such district or part of a district."

" 3. By a supervisor in refusing to pay any such moneys to any such district."

" 4. By the trustees of any district in paying or refusing to pay any teacher, or in refusing to admit any scholar gratuitously into any school."

" 5. By any trustees of any school library concerning such library, or the books therein or the use of such books."

" 6. By any district meeting in relation to the library."

" 7. By any other official act or decision concerning any other matter under this Act, or any other Act pertaining to common schools." [1]

All such appeals the State Superintendent of Public Instruction is "authorized and required to examine and decide . . . and his decision shall be final and conclusive, and not subject to question or review in any place or court whatever."

---

[1] *Consolidated School Law.* Title xiv. From 1841 to 1847 the County Superintendents heard appeals in the first instance, and only after their decisions could the matter come to the State Superintendent. In 5 *Howard's Practice Reports,* p. 417 (1851), it was held that the Free School Act (1849) repealed the appellate jurisdiction of the State Superintendent; but in 1853 it was restored by the Legislature (c. 78).

The appellate jurisdiction of the State Superintendent does not debar a plaintiff from bringing action in the courts, provided he does so before appealing to the State Superintendent; but where any such action is brought against school officers for any act performed by them by virtue of or under color of their offices, *which might have been the subject of an appeal to the Superintendent,* no costs are allowed to the plaintiff where the court certifies that it appeared on the trial that the defendants acted in good faith.

These provisions were intended, to quote the opinion of the Supreme Court, "as a cheap and expeditious mode of settling most if not all of the difficulties and disputes arising in the course of the execution of the law organizing and regulating common schools. The legislature has virtually declared that where a party will forego that convenient method of adjusting such a controversy . . . and resort to the ordinary courts, it shall be at his own expense as regards costs." [1]   The same view of the scope of this power is taken by the Court of Appeals. The grant of appellate jurisdiction to the State Superintendent "is broad and comprehensive in its terms, and evidently includes any and all acts which may possibly arise in regard to the official proceedings of these [school] officers . . . The legislature no doubt intended to prevent needless prosecutions and unnecessary suits against officers of this character, who had acted in good faith in the discharge of their official duties." [2]

[1] 3 *Denio*, 175; similar opinions given earlier in 2 *Wendell*, 287, and 11 *Wendell*, 91.

[2] 38 *New York Reports*, 58 (1868).

In People *vs.* Martin (Monroe County Supreme Court, 1855) Judge Welles held that appeals to the State Superintendent could only be taken on *acts* of local authorities, and not on questions involving their discretion, such as certifying to moral character of a candidate for teacher. He was not, however, supported in this opinion by the other two judges, and the decision rested on other grounds. 21 *Barbour*, 252.

The courts have also on several occasions declined to review the action of the State Superintendent on appeal cases,
in obedience to the provisions of the statute that his decision
"shall be final and conclusive and not subject to question or
review in any court whatever."[1]   In one of these cases, the
Judge raised the query whether the appellate jurisdiction of
the State Superintendent was not unconstitutional, because it
did not provide a trial by jury.[2]   However, in this case the
defendant by acquiescing in the jurisdiction of the State
Superintendent had waived his right to a jury trial, and the
question did not have to be decided by that court.   The
fact that this argument has not been used in subsequent
cases, the other decisions accepting the law as constitutional,
and the long established exercise of the appellate jurisdiction, together establish a strong presumption against this
power of the State Superintendent being overthrown by the
courts.

The authority of the State Superintendent over appeals
includes the regulation of the procedure.   Under this power,
rules of practice have been established,[3] requiring the appeals
to be in writing, with the testimony in the form of affidavits;
a copy of the appeal must be served on the officer whose
act or decision is complained of, and the officer must answer
within ten days.   The decision of the Superintendent can
dispose of all the questions connected with the case, reverse
a wrong proceeding and also direct the appropriate remedy,
so as to afford redress to all persons who have been injuri-
ously affected.   In these respects, the appeal to the State
Superintendent is preferable to a common law action, which

[1] People *vs.* Collins (1867), 34 *How. Pr.,* 336; People *vs.* Draper, (1892), 63
Hun., 389; People *vs.* Eckler, (1880), 19 *Hun.,* 609.

[2] 19 *Hun.,* 609.   Smith, in 34 *How. Pr.* (1867), had said: "I have no doubt
this is a valid act, and that the legislature had ample power to pass it."

[3] Rules of Practice in *School Code* (1887), 123-4.

inures only to the benefit of the person who brings it, and gives to him pecuniary damages only, without substituting a correct proceeding in the place of an erroneous one.[1]

The State Superintendent can enforce his decisions against any school officer by exercising his power of removal or by withholding the district's share of the State grant.[2] In the case of supervisors, or town clerks, the only method of enforcement is by application to the Supreme Court for a mandamus. In general, however, there is no need of compulsory action, as the decisions are submitted to without objection.

The effective authority of the State Superintendent's appellate jurisdiction is shown not so much by the text of the law, or the language of judicial decisions, as by the actual use made of the powers conferred, Judged by the number of appeals, and the questions involved, the powers actually exercised by the State Superintendent are seen to be fully as comprehensive as those conferred in the statute. As early as 1836, Secretary of State Dix declared that the duty of determining appeal cases was the most important and arduous of his functions as Superintendent of Schools.[3] For the last forty years, the number of appeal cases annually decided has averaged over a hundred. The decisions of the most important cases are annually published in the State Superintendent's Report; and the Code of Public Instruction contains a digest of the decisions of over 300 pages, which, no less than the statutes, guide the school officers throughout the State in the discharge of their duties. The scope of the authority of the State Superintendent may be shown by a consideration of the character of questions which are in-

---

[1] *Report of State Superintendent of Public Instruction* xlii, 33.

[2] People *vs.* Allen, 78 *New York State Reporter*, 566.

[3] *Report of Superintendent of Common Schools*, xxiv, 31.

volved in these appeal cases, with some indications as to the general policy shown in the decisions.

Many cases are brought which concern the action or inaction of school commissioners   In those concerned with the formation, alteration or dissolution of school districts, the policy of the State Superintendents has been to favor consolidation and to discountenance the formation of weak districts.   Annulments or refusals to grant teacher's certificate are not sustained if made on trivial charges or without a proper inquiry.   In matters involving the approval of schoolhouse sites, and plans for heating, lighting and ventilating school buildings, and the condemnation of school buildings, the policy has been to leave more to the discretion of the commissioners; but where abuse of this discretion is shown their actions will be vacated.

The cases concerned with the proceedings of school district meetings are much more numerous and perplexing; they involve questions as to the legality of elections, of votes ordering the levy of taxes, the designation or purchase of school house sites, and the construction of school houses. The entire proceedings of a meeting are frequently set aside by the State Superintendent on account of lack of proper notice, precipitancy in organization, or turbulence and disorder; and a decision by a close vote at a meeting held on a stormy night has been re-opened.   The selection of an unsanitary site for a school house has been set aside, and the delegation of the power of selection is not permitted.   Tax votes must name specific objects, and an exorbitant appropriation for any object will be set aside; if no tax is voted the trustees have been directed to levy a tax.   Purely technical omissions are not, however, allowed to void the proceedings of a district meeting,—such as bad spelling in the notice or the neglect to send notice to every taxpayer.

The appeals against the acts and decisions of school trustees form another large class of cases which come before the State Superintendent. The regulation of studies and choice of text-books are left to the discretion of the trustees, except when the latter is limited by the statute prohibiting changes oftener than once in five years. The use of buildings for other than school purposes is also left to the discretion of trustees, though their use by secret societies is not approved. Questions of residence involving the right to attend school have been decided against the trustees, and also the exclusion of colored children where no special school is provided for them.

The employment and dismissal of teachers leads to a vast number of cases, and certain general principles are now laid down. The pay of teachers must continue if school is closed during the contract period on account of an epidemic, fire, or the attendance of the teacher at a teachers' institute. Contracts must be for a reasonable length of time; janitor's work is not included in a contract to teach; dismissals must be for cause specified, and the holder of a state certificate cannot be removed (even by a city superintendent) until the state certificate is annulled either by the State Superintendent or by the city board of education. The exclusive employment of members of a particular organization (sisters of charity) for a particular school, and the wearing of the garb of the organization by the teachers on duty, has been ordered discontinued.

Cases against city boards of education are not so frequent as those against district trustees; but the jurisdiction of the State Superintendent over boards organized by special Act has been distinctly asserted and recognized. In one such instance, it was held that the failure of a city council to levy the school tax did not justify the board of education in closing the schools, since the city was liable for the expenses

which could be collected by due process of law.[1]   In another
recent case, where the dispute between the two halves of a
bi-partisan board of education left the city schools unpro-
vided for, the State Superintendent appointed a city superintendent and teachers and opened the schools.   This action
was sustained by the Supreme Court on the ground that it
was the function of the State to see that the schools are
maintained.[2]

Besides the many cases against local school officials,
appeals have also been made to the State Superintendent
against disciplinary regulations of teachers; and his decisions on these establish rules for even this detail of school
management.   Cruel and unusual punishments are repre-
hended; expulsions for leaving the school grounds during
recess, or for a more serious breach of discipline which was
the result of momentary impulse, have been disallowed.
Fines, even if imposed by the trustees, are not permitted.
On the other hand, appeals to secure the discontinuance of
corporal punishment have not been successful.

From these illustrations of the subject matter of appeals
and the decisions of the State Superintendent, it will be evident that through his appellate jurisdiction he exercises an
extensive control over local school management and administration throughout the State.   This form of authority does
not, however, give him control over the entire field of educational administration; and there remain to be noticed
some other methods by which he influences and directs the
common school system.   These methods include the advisory influence over the construction of school buildings
and the curriculum of instruction, the supervision of the
enforcement of the Compulsory Attendance Law, and the

[1] Elmira Board of Education, *Decisions* nos. 3990 and 3993 (1890).

[2] *Educational Review*, xv, 100, 111.

much more highly centralized control over the education and examination of teachers for the public schools.

As has been indicated, the State Superintendent has no direct authority or control over the course of study in schools, or over the construction of school buildings. Nevertheless, within recent years, he has come to wield a considerable advisory and educational influence in such matters. Acting under the provisions of a statute of 1887, a pamphlet of architects' designs for school-houses, with suggestions as to lighting, warming and ventilating school buildings and preparing grounds, was published under the supervision of the state department, and distributed freely to local authorities. On a design being selected by a local board of education, the state department furnishes working plans and estimates for the building desired.[1] The practical benefit derived from the publication has been shown by the numerous calls on the department for working plans, by applications from other States for the pamphlet of designs, and by the request of the United States Commissioner of Education to republish the book as one of his circulars of information. To supplement this book, the late reports of the State Superintendent contain exhibits of views and plans of school buildings erected in the State, selected so as to show the best suggestions for buildings of different types and cost of construction. These illustrative pamphlets must be of very material help to school boards, furnishing them with information as to the latest improvements of use in meeting the problem of school construction.

It is only within recent years that any active attempt has been made to regulate the course of study in district schools so as to prevent the interruption and retrogression resulting from frequent changes of teachers, and to secure some uni

---

[1] *Report of Superintendent of Public Instruction*, xxxv, 59.

formity of purpose in the various schools. The first action was taken some fifteen years ago, when certain school commissioners prepared and recommended an outline course of study for grammar grades. This course was improved in several revisions, suggestions on classification and methods were added, the system received the sanction of the State association of school commissioners, and by voluntary adoption went into use in about ninety commissioner districts. In 1895 the State Superintendent was requested to undertake the supervision of this matter, and in the following year a new edition was issued by the state department. The suggested courses of study are only in outline, leaving much to the teacher's experience and discretion, and no attempt is made to establish any rigid system. Nevertheless, this extension of the State Superintendent's jurisdiction, even if only an advisory influence, is of some importance. There can be little doubt that the official position given to the course of study will cause its more general adoption, and thus tend to establish closer relations and a more uniform system among the public schools. At the same time, the absence of any compulsory provision should ·prevent the adoption of methods not adapted to local conditions.

Some legislative regulations on the subjects to be studied in the common schools should be here noticed. In 1875[1] the teaching of free-hand drawing was made compulsory in all schools in cities and union districts; and at the same time training in manual arts was authorized. In 1893[2] the study of vocal music in the public schools and teachers' institutes was authorized. A more rigid requirement is that prescribing a course of study in hygiene and physiology, with special reference to the effects of alcohol and other narcotics on the human system. This was first required in 1880, but

---

[1] *Laws of* 1875, c. 322.　　　　　[2] *Ibid.*, 1896, c. 636.

in 1896 another law enacted much more detailed regulations on this subject.[1] By the later statute, the subject must be studied every year in the course, with three lessons a week for ten weeks in each year; a series of graded books must be used, and examinations given each year. This detailed legislation is due to moral sentiment on a particular subject, and is in no sense indicative of any tendency toward general legislative regulation and interference in the courses of study; but it may be pointed out that the same considerations which make any legislative regulation of the general school curriculum inadvisable apply with equal force to the detailed regulation of this particular subject. The serious objections to a rigid system of instruction for the entire State, even if prepared by experienced and expert officers in the State department, become more pronounced when the legislature, in the midst of its many and conflicting duties, attempts to frame minute provisions as to the number of hours of instruction, the character of text-books to be used, examinations, etc., and imposes this *iron-clad* system on every school in the state. Another method of legislative action is seen in the provisions for instruction in natural history, geography, and kindred subjects, made in 1897.[2] An appropriation of $15,000 for this purpose is made, to be used for illustrated lectures on these subjects, to be given under the direction of the State Superintendent.

The Compulsory Education Law of 1894 contained important advances over the former ineffective law of 1874. Parents are made responsible for the non-attendance of their children at school; cities and villages are required to provide school attendance officers to enforce the law, and the State Superintendent is authorized to employ assistants to investigate the extent to which the act is carried out. The

---

[1] *Laws of* 1896, c. 901.   [2] *Ibid.*, 1897, c. 790.

inspectors appointed under this provision have no compulsory powers; but on their investigations and reports the
State Superintendent can withhold from any district not
obeying the law one-half of its quota of the State appropriation for common schools. The reports of these inspectors[1]
show that New York City appoints twenty school attendance
officers, four other cities have from five to nine officers, four
cities have two, and twenty-nine cities have one officer each;
Brooklyn, Rochester and Syracuse have provided Truant
Schools, and other cities have special classes for truants.
In the four years since the Act went into effect the total
enrollment at the common schools has increased by 120,-
000, and the average attendance by 130,000. The previous
four years showed an increase of only 50,000; while for the
twelve years before 1889, there had been no increase in the
total enrollment, and the annual increase in average attendance had been only about 6,000.[2] There is still room for
much improvement before anything like a full attendance of
children will be secured; but one result of the investigations
of the State inspectors has been to attract attention to the
fact that in twenty-one of the cities in the State, the school
accommodations were not sufficient for those who attend
voluntarily. This knowledge, through force of public sentiment, is compelling the local authorities to provide the
necessary schools, without which compulsory attendance is
impracticable.

[1] *Report of the State Superintendent of Public Instruction*, xliii., 1002.

	Enrollment.	Average Attendance.
1872	1,024,130	494,850
1876	1,067,190	541,610
1881	1,021,282	559,399
1885	1,024,845	611,019
1889	1,033,813	637,487
1893	1,083,228	688,097
1897	1,203,199	820,254

The education and examination of teachers for the public schools are now carried on under the supervision of the State Superintendent to a much greater extent than any other part of the school system. This power is exercised through the system of uniform teachers' examinations, the direction of teachers' institutes, and the supervision of normal schools and teachers' training classes in high schools and academies.

The examination and licensing of teachers for the public schools has been, and is now in form, a function of the school commissioners. The State Superintendent has also the right to examine and grant certificates; but these State certificates, being for life, have been placed on a much higher standard than the commissioner examinations, and only a small number of teachers have applied for them. Before 1887 the commissioner examinations were conducted independently, each commissioner choosing his subjects, and having his own method of examination and marking the results. In that year, the State Superintendent attempted to secure the passage of a law providing for uniform examinations; but this failing in the legislature, the department, at the request of a number of commissioners, prepared a series of uniform question papers.[1] These were used that year by 65 commissioners, and in the following year all of the commissioners had voluntarily adopted the new system.[2] This secured uniformity in questions and written examinations for all teachers; but as the answers were still examined and marked by the various commissioners, certificates from different commissioners had still a widely different value. In 1893, however, the State department called in and marked all the papers of candidates for first grade (five year) certificates, and in 1894 an increased appropriation

[1] *Report of the State Superintendent of Public Instruction*, xxxiv, 22.

[2] *Ibid.*, xxxv, 32.

for the department made possible the appointment of a State board of examiners to examine and mark all the papers.[1] At the same time, the authority of the State Superintendent was confirmed by a clause in the Consolidated School Act, providing that commissioners' examinations should be under rules and regulations prescribed by the Superintendent of Public Instruction. The uniform system of examinations has also been voluntarily adopted in 24 of the cities in the State.[2] The work of the examination division of the Department of Public Instruction consists in preparing different series of question papers for three grades of examinations, and of examining and marking the papers of over 20,000 candidates a year. Of these candidates over 50 per cent. fail to obtain certificates.

The State Superintendents have been unanimous in testifying to the beneficial results of the uniform system of examinations. " It has led every person desiring to enter the teaching service to know that the first requisite qualification of the teacher is scholarship . . . It has placed the work of teachers upon a professional basis and given the calling added respect and dignity."[3] Indirectly this system of uniform teachers' examinations has served to introduce a graded course of study in a large number of rural schools, and in other ways its influence broadens and makes more useful the work of these schools.

The management of the teachers' institutes in the various commissioner districts is now almost completely in the hands of the State department. The instruction is given by members of the State corps of institute conductors and special instructors, according to a definite program furnished in advance to the teachers. Over a hundred institutes are held each year, with an aggregate attendance of 16,000 teachers;

---

[1] *Report of the State Superintendent of Public Instruction*, xl, 32; xli, 30.
[2] *Ibid.*, xliii, 23.　　　　　　　　　　[3] *Ibid.*, xlii, 20.

and there can be no question that the instruction given in subject-matter and methods of teaching, as well as the new life and inspiration received by the teachers, has far-reaching results in improving the work of the schools. Incidentally, the institutes serve other purposes; through them the State department is kept in touch with all the educational forces of the State, while the evening lectures given at the institutes are a means of educating and interesting the public in educational matters.

The appointment of the local board for each of the normal schools in the State would of itself give the Superintendent of Public Instruction a large authority over their management, although the necessity for securing the consent of the Chancellor of the University to a removal might serve as a limitation. But the direct authority of the State Superintendent extends to many other matters than the appointment of the local boards. The course of study adopted by the local boards must secure his approval; he determines the number of teachers to be employed and their wages, he fixes the number of pupils and the method of selection, and grants diplomas.

The direction of teachers' training classes in high schools and academies, transferred to the State Superintendent in 1889, gives him an equal if not a greater authority over the education of teachers in these institutions. The State Superintendent names the schools and academies to which the State appropriation for special instruction to teachers will be apportioned, prescribes the conditions of admission to such training classes, the course of instruction, and the regulations under which the instruction shall be given. Such training classes are also subject to inspection by the State department, two special inspectors being employed for this purpose. Since the transfer of the supervision of these classes from the Regents of the University, the number of

PUBLIC EDUCATION

classes increased from 49, with 758 pupils, to 140, with 2500 pupils, in 1894–5. The adoption of higher requirements for admission in 1895–6, however, cut down these last figures by more than one-half. The graduates from these training classes and normal schools are licensed to teach without passing the special teacher's examinations; and the number of such teachers is constantly increasing. In 1864, 300 teachers were graduates of these institutions; in 1881 there were 1100; and in 1896, nearly 4000 out of a total of 28,500 teachers were of this class.

The extension of the State Superintendent's control over the training of teachers for city schools, which went into effect in 1897, is of no little importance. Under this law[1] no new teacher can be employed in any city school who has not had three years successful experience in teaching, or has graduated from a high school or academy having a course of study of not less than three years prescribed by the State Superintendent, and has also graduated from a course in practical and theoretical pedagogy of not less than thirty-eight weeks, approved by the State Superintendent. Under this law, the State Superintendent has prepared a minimum three years' course of study, which must be adopted by all high schools and academies whose graduates wish to teach in any city schools.

Through this wide control over the education and the examination of teachers the Department of Public Instruction can and does exercise a profound influence over the character of the instruction in all the public schools of the State.

The Superintendent of Public Instruction also exercises some important functions over matters not directly part of the common school system, but closely connected therewith. He is charged with providing schools for the Indian children

---

[1] *Laws of* 1895, c. 1031.

in the State, and appointing superintendents for the same. He has the duty of visiting and inspecting all the institutions in the State for the instruction of the deaf and dumb, and blind, and of suggesting improvements in their instruction and discipline; he also has the power of appointing State pupils to these various institutions. Finally the State Superintendent is *ex-officio* a regent of the University of the State of New York, a trustee of Cornell University, and of the New York State Asylum for Idiots.

This discussion of the functions and authority of the State Superintendent of Public Instruction must have demonstrated that in practice as well as in legal theory, "education is not city, village, county or town business. It is a matter belonging to the State government."[1] Nevertheless, through the continued use of local officers and the traditions of earlier days, there are still traces of the opinion that educational affairs are matters of purely local concern for each community to manage or mismanage as it pleases. It may be well therefore to note the principles on which State supervision and control are founded.

The exercise of State authority may be justified on the ground that the power of taxation, the essential element in any system of public education, is a State power, and the localities can exercise it only so far as conferred by the State.[2] The State may, therefore, fairly claim that it must see that this power of taxation is properly used by the localities and yields the results for which the grant of power has been made. This principle would justify State supervision of all local taxation and expenditure; but where the functions of local government concern only the localities, and where mismanagement results mainly in pecuniary loss which falls on the community responsible for the mistakes, State control

[1] Judge Gaynor, in *New York State Reporter*, vol. 72; p. 155.
[2] A. S. Draper, in *Educational Review*, i, 30.

has not as yet been introduced.   With school administration,
however, this is not the case.   The loss falls on more than
the locality immediately concerned, and affects the intellectual virility and moral powers of the whole people.[1]   In the
words of the Massachusetts Constitution, " knowledge and
and learning, as well as virtue, generally diffused throughout
the community, are essential to the preservation of a free
government, and of the rights and liberties of the people."
Acting on this principle, the State not only authorizes local
taxation, but also uses part of the State revenue for the support of the schools.   To see that this State grant is used
wisely, and that the schools it helps to maintain provide the
quality of instruction which the State grant is meant to
secure are reasonable grounds for the.extent of State control
exercised.

It should, however, be noticed that the system of State
supervision in no way restricts the local authorities in adding
to their educational arrangements.   It is a control exercised
to bring the schools throughout the State up to a minimum
standard ; beyond that, the local officials are free to extend
their school system to any degree.   In the cities such extensions are generally made, and for that reason there is less
occasion for the exercise of the State Superintendent's authority; but, as we have seen, when occasion arises his
powers are not limited by the fact that city boards of education hold their powers under special statutes.

It is not possible to measure accurately the total results
due to the central control now exercised over the common
school system of New York State.   On the one hand, other
causes than central control have operated to produce the
present situation, and on the other hand much of the improvement cannot be described in any mathematical terms.

[1] *Educational Review,* xv, 109.

We have, however, seen the recent improvement in school attendance which has appeared since the enactment of the Compulsory Education Law. Statistics of illiteracy may also serve as an indication of how far the fundamental task in public education is being met; and the following table shows the conditions in New York State at the last three decennial censuses:

	Total Popula-tion.	Illiter-ates over 10 years of age.	Per cent. illiterate.	Illiter-ates 10 to 20 years of age.	Native-born Popula-tion.	Native-born il-literates over 10 years of age.	Per cent. native-born il-literates.
1870....	4,382,759	239,271	5.84	40,533	3,244,406	70,702	2.18
1880....	5,082,871	219,600	4.32	27,416	3,871,492	70,941	1.83
1890....	5,997,843	266,911	4.45	23,889	4,426,804	68,755	1.55

The columns for the total population include illiterate foreigners, most of whom have grown to manhood beyond the reach of the public school system. In the columns for children between ten and twenty years of age and for native-born population there is seen to be not only a relative decline in the proportion of illiterates, but also an absolute decrease in the number of persons unable to read.

Much of the advance in educational lines which has produced these results must be ascribed to the authority and activity of the State department. Even where its authority has not been directly exercised much is due to it. Through the State officials educational improvements have been brought to the attention of backward localities, and have thus been more widely used than if there had been no State agency. Moreover, the concentration of educational activity has served to attract public attention to the importance and needs of the schools; and this has been an important factor in securing the large increments of local taxation without which no such rapid development could have been made. These results are not capable of statistical demonstration; but that central control is responsible, directly and indirectly, for a vast deal of recent educational advance is shown by the unanimity of opinion among educators, and by the ready acceptance of the steadily increasing authority of the State department.

II. THE UNIVERSITY OF THE STATE OF NEW YORK.

Origin of the Regents of the University. State supervision of institutions for secondary and higher education was established in New York before the beginnings of the Common School system; and the State organ provided has continued as a separate authority, exercising its control independently of the State Superintendent of Public Instruction, and on widely different principles. During the early part of the eighteenth century several acts were passed by the New York provincial assembly establishing academies and King's college;[1] but these were not the result of any well-defined policy, and were accompanied by no central control over the institutions. The beginning of more systematic action was brought about by the necessity of reorganizing the college, which during the Revolutionary War had practically disbanded. In 1784, a corporation was created, termed the Regents of the University of the State of New York, composed of the principal State officers and fifty-seven other persons named by the legislature. This body succeeded to all the corporate rights of King's College, whose name was now changed to Columbia College, and it was further authorized to establish additional schools and col-

[1] *Colonial Laws of New York*, chaps. 120, 594, 658, 840, 860, 909.

leges in the State, which should together form the University
of the State of New York, under the control of the Regents.[1]

Three years' experience revealed certain defects in this
scheme. No new colleges were created, and the hopes of
those who had looked for a comprehensive system of educational institutions in different parts of the State were disap-
pointed. At the same time, the control of the Regents over
the government of Columbia College had proven inconvenient.
The large number of regents made full meetings impossible;
and, while the Columbia men in New York city could
ordinarily control the meetings of the board, there was
always friction between them and the rural members. The
result of this mutual dissatisfaction was a reorganization of
the system in 1787.[2] A separate Board of Trustees was
established for the management of Columbia College. The
Regents were continued as a supervisory authority over all
the colleges and academies in the State; the number of
members was reduced to nineteen, elected for life by the
legislature, with the Governor and Lieutenant-Governor of
the State as *ex officio* members.[3]

The principles of the law of 1787 have been followed in
all later legislation in reference to higher education in New
York. The immediate management of each institution has
been left to its own board of trustees or other local officers,
and in the case of the colleges this independence has been
almost complete. Over the academies and high schools,
however, the Regents exercise a general oversight and control. In form, the University is a system of federated institutions, and the board of Regents is a private corporation

---

[1] *Laws of* 1784, c. 51.

[2] A full discussion of the early history of the Regents is given in S. Sherwood:
University of the State of New York, published as *Regents' Bulletin* for 1893
No. 11.

[3] *Laws of* 1787, c. 82.

chartered by the State. In fact, the Regents constitute a State bureau of higher education, with powers of supervision over private and local institutions, and also with some powers of direct administration.

The work of the Regents has increased steadily with the growth of the State, and there also have been some changes in their methods and additions to their powers. Especially within the last decade their field of activities has been broadened and their supervision of schools has become more effective. This development can, however, be better noted in connection with their various forms of action, than in a continuous sketch of the entire history.

Incorporation of Institutions. Under the authority to incorporate colleges and academies, the Regents of the University early established certain conditions requiring a suitable equipment and endowment of proposed institutions before granting charters. These rules have prevented the establishment of weak and temporary enterprises, and have also checked the ambition of academies which aspired to the dignity of colleges. The first college chartered by the Regents was Union, in 1795; no other applications were granted until 1812, when Hamilton College was incorporated; and in 1822, a college charter was bestowed on Geneva Academy. Charters to academies were, of course, more numerous. Two were granted in 1787; by 1800, nineteen academies had been chartered; and by 1820, forty-eight charters had been issued.[1] Some of these, however, failed to comply with the conditions imposed, and others had been discontinued. In 1820, thirty were reported to the legislature as making returns and receiving their share of the State grants.

The restrictions established by the Regents on the issuance of charters caused many proposed institutions to turn to the legislature. The Constitution of 1821, con-

[1] Hough, *Historical and Statistical Record*, p. 28.

tained a clause requiring the assent of two-thirds of the members of each house of the legislature for the passage of any act creating a corporation. The question whether this abrogated the powers of the Regents was raised, and although never clearly settled, the legislature began to exercise its power of granting special charters. Between 1819 and 1830 more than forty academic charters were granted by the legislature, and in the next decade a still greater number, in most of which no conditions were imposed.[1] In 1831, the University of the City of New York was chartered by the legislature, and for the next forty years most of the new colleges were incorporated by the legislature.

After 1840, legislative charters to academies became much less frequent, and new institutions received their authorization from the Regents, who, in 1851, established fixed regulations for such charters. In 1853, their power to grant charters was affirmed and extended. An act of that year required the Regents, to establish general rules prescribing the conditions for the incorporation of any institution of learning, and authorizing them for cause shown to annul, alter or amend any charter granted by them. Power to incorporate medical colleges was also specifically granted.[2]

In 1892, the Regents were given exclusive power to grant charters to educational institutions, and any such institution which discontinues educational operations is required to surrender its charter. Since the grant of this power, the Regents have adopted a standard form of charter.[3] The former system of accepting charters drawn up by the applicants had produced the same confusion and uncertainty as

[1] Of 435 charters granted before 1865, 213 were by the legislature and 222 were by the Regents; 61 of the former and 104 of the latter were extinct in 1865. *Reports of the Regents*, vol. 80, p. 274.

[2] *Laws of* 1853, c. 184.

[3] *Reports of the Regents*, vol. 107, p. 122.

to powers granted to colleges and academies, as exists in reference to municipal corporations. Under the new system a simple and uniform charter is issued to all institutions. These charters are, moreover, granted only after personal examination by agents of the board, to make certain that suitable equipment and ample provision for the support of the proposed institution has been provided.

The early charters were all granted to private institutions, supported by private endowment and tuition fees, and managed by a private board of trustees. The Union Free School law of 1853[1] authorized the establishment of academical departments in the union district free schools, and provided that whenever an academy existed within a district it might be transferred to the trustees of the union district. The academical departments in these tax-supported schools were subject to the same supervision by the Regents as the private academies, and received their share of the State grants on the same basis.

The transition from endowed academies to tax-supported high schools was not rapid at first. By 1871, there were only 45 of the latter to 164 of the former in operation. Since then, however, there has been a steady abandonment of the academies and a constant increase in the number of free high schools, and in the last ten years the addition to the latter class has been especially rapid. From 1888 to 1896 there was an apparent growth in the number of academies, but this was due to a number of long-established Roman Catholic institutions connecting themselves with the University. Even with this addition, the number of academies on the Regents' list in 1897 was but 119 with 9500 students, to 464 tax-supported high schools with 44,000 students.[2] Of the higher institutions of learning connected with the Univer-

[1] *Laws of* 1853, c. 433.

[2] *Reports of the Regents*, vol. 102, p. 36; vol. 111, p. 68.

sity, there are 34 colleges with 8000 students, and 71 professional and technical schools with nearly 20,000 students.

Distribution of State Aid. State grants to the colleges
have in all cases been made directly to the particular institutions without the intervention of the Regents. The first
grants to the academies were similarly made; but in 1790
the legislature authorized the Regents to lease certain State
lands, and to apply the rents and profits to the academies.
In 1793, the first apportionment was made to the ten
academies then in the University,[1] and in 1794 £1500 was
distributed among twelve academies.[2] In 1813 the proceeds
from certain land sales were to be invested and the interest
distributed by the Regents, and the Literature Fund thus established was afterward increased from other sources. The
principle of distribution was changed from time to time. In
1817, a general regulation was made by the Regents that
future apportionments should be in proportion to the number of students pursuing the branches of study preparatory
to "well-regulated colleges." In the law of 1827, it was
directed that the basis should be the number of pupils "who
shall have pursued classical studies or the higher branches
of English education or both." The Revised Statutes which
went into effect in 1830 required the Regents, in the first
place, to divide the amount equally among the eight senatorial districts, and this plan, although obviously unfair and
opposed by the Regents, was continued for nearly twenty
years.

Up to 1832, part of the securities constituting the Literature Fund had been held by the Comptroller, and the income
from these investments had been appropriated by the legislature to such academies as had the most influence. In
1832 all the securities were transferred to the custody of the

[1] *Reports of the Regents,* vol. 107, p. 53.
[2] Hough, *Historical and Statistical Record,* p. 31.

Comptroller, and the distribution of all the income was assigned to the Regents.[1] On the receipt of the United States deposit, in 1837, a part of the interest from this fund was assigned to the academies, increasing the total annual appropriation from $10,000 to $40,000. Perhaps the larger amount of State aid made more evident the unfairness of the rigid system of equal distribution by senatorial districts, for in 1847 this requirement in the statute was omitted.[2]

The adoption of the system of Regents' preliminary examinations, in 1865,[3] made possible a more uniform standard in apportioning the State grants, but did not change the principles of distribution. After 1880, however, the distribution was based in part on certificates granted to those who passed Regents' examinations in advanced or academic subjects, and only the balance of the State appropriation was awarded according to the attendance of those who had passed the preliminary examinations.

The State grant of $40,000 a year, fixed in 1837, remained unchanged for fifty years. Meanwhile the number of academies had trebled, the number of scholars had quadrupled, and the expenditure of the academies had multiplied sevenfold. This increasing divisor with a constant dividend had the effect of decreasing the amount to each school, and considering the total expenditures, the State grant became insignificant. Accordingly, in 1887, an appropriation of $60,000 was added to the $12,000 from the Literature Fund and the $40,000 from the United States Deposit Fund.

This increase was, however, soon made insignificant by the enormous development in secondary education which set in at this time. Within the next eight years the number of high schools and academies had almost doubled again,

---

[1] *Laws of* 1832, c. 8.

[2] *Laws of* 1847, c. 258.

[3] See p. 68.

and their expenditures had increased 250 per cent.[1] The increase in the number of students who passed the advanced examinations was so large that the amount apportioned on this basis almost equaled the total appropriation, and the payment for the number of academic scholars in attendance was reduced, until in 1893 it was only one-fifth of a cent for each student. To meet this situation, the Horton Law of 1895[2] provided for a quota of $100 to each school, with one cent for each day's attendance of each academic student, $5 for each regular academic certificate issued, and $5 extra for each student's first diploma or college entrance certificate. Instead of a fixed amount, the annual appropriation would vary so as to meet these conditions, and in practice the effect has been almost to double the amount of State aid to the academies. In 1897 the total grants amounted to $193,000.[3]

Reports and Visitations. The Board of Regents is authorized, by its officers, committees and agents, to visit and inspect all the colleges and academies in the State; and each of these institutions is required to make an annual report of its affairs to the Regents. As early as 1804, a system of printed blanks for detailed reports came into use; but after four years the reports became very brief, simply stating the numbers in attendance at the colleges, the number graduating, and as to the academies that their affairs were "in a flourishing condition."[4]   In 1835 fuller reports

	Academies and High Schools.	No. of Scholars.	Total Expenditures.
1839	118	10,881	$208,864
1887	294	39,523	1,383,609
1895	498	49,937	3,133,218
1897	583	53,464	3,284,246

[2] *Laws of* 1895, c. 341.

[3] *Reports of the Regents*, vol. III, p. 84.

[4] Hough: *Historical and Statistical Record*, p. 70.

from the colleges and academies began to be published, and
since that time the series of educational statistics is un-
broken. With the later development, the details become
more complete, accurate and systematic, giving information
upon the financial resources, expenditure, courses of instruction, apparatus, teachers and students in each institution. These reports when printed make an annual volume
of over 1000 pages, while the more important facts are
summarized and abridged in carefully prepared abstracts and
statistical tables.

The early reports of the Regents contain no records of
systematic visitations of the schools under their supervision;
but beginning in 1858 a list of the visitations by the Regents
and Secretary in the previous year is presented in the
reports to the legislature.[1] After 1882, visitations were also
made by the inspector of teachers' training classes, then
under the supervision of the Regents; but on the transfer of
this duty to the Superintendent of Public Instruction, in
1889, this method of making personal examinations of the
academies was no longer possible. The value of a systematic visitation of the academies by an officer of the University was by this time realized, and in 1890 an inspector
of schools was appointed[2] to visit the schools, inform himself of their condition or needs, and make suggestions for
improvement. Additional inspectors have since been appointed, so that each school might be visited at least once a
year. The inspection system was placed on a more secure
basis by the University Law of 1892, which forbids the
Regents to apportion the State grants to institutions which
have not been personally inspected by an officer of the University. In 1896 there were six inspectors, who made in all
915 visits during the year. The inspectors have no com-

[1] *Reports of the Regents*, vol. 71, p. 18.
[2] *Report of the Regents*, vol. 104, p. 15.

pulsory authority; but their advice and suggestions are well received, and their visits much appreciated by the local principals and directors. The result of six years' experience with this system of inspection has confirmed the Regents' opinion of the advantages it secures in improving the schools and academies.

Academic Examinations. The early system of determining the number of qualified scholars, for the apportionment of the State grants, was the simple method of accepting the reports of the academies. Under this system it was to the self-interest of each academy to lower its standards, as in this way it could report a larger number of qualified scholars, and receive a larger share of the State moneys. To counteract this tendency, and also to secure a uniform standard on which to have an equitable apportionment, the Regents, in 1865, arranged simultaneous written examinations in all the institutions under their care.[1] The examinations were in arithmetic, English grammar, geography, and spelling; and only those who could show a fair knowledge of these preliminary subjects were after this accepted as academic scholars. The first result of these examinations was a reduction in the number of academic scholars, from 21,947 claimed in 1865 to less than 6,000. This showing had the natural effect of causing the academies to improve their standards and methods of instruction; and in consequence the number of successful candidates has steadily increased. From 1890 to 1896 the number securing these certificates, which mark the completion of the grammar school courses, increased 128 per cent., while the attendance at the common schools had increased but 12 per cent.[2]

The success of the practical supervision over the academies exercised by these examinations in preliminary subjects led

[1] *Reports of the Regents,* vol. 79, p. 18.

[2] *Reports of the Regents,* vol. 110, p. 73.

the legislature, in 1877, to authorize the extension of the system to more advanced or academic studies.[1] In 1880, the future distribution of the State grants was made dependent in part upon the examinations in these higher subjects. Regents' certificates were issued to those who passed the examinations, and Regents' diplomas to those who passed in a number of subjects determined as the standard for a high school course. The influence of these advanced examinations and certificates was beneficial in the highest degree. They made clear to many schools weak points not evident so long as their results were tested only by defective local standards. With improved methods and additional courses of studies came the demand for further extensions of the Regents' examinations; and additions were made after careful comparison of views between the Regents and the schools. In 1878, examinations were offered in twenty subjects; by 1896 the number had been increased to eighty.[2] The number of candidates for the examinations has also increased at an even more rapid rate. In 1865 there were 20,000 examination papers; in 1880 there were over 80,000, and in 1896 nearly 400,000. The number of papers allowed by the Regents averages about 60 per cent. of the number of papers written.

Dr. William T. Harris, the United States Commissioner of Education, has said of the results of this system: " The Regents have proved that a state examining board can exercise a stimulating, elevating and unifying influence upon hundreds of institutions of secondary education scattered over a large state, and can wield that power with machinery which, considering the scale of operations, may fairly be called simple and inexpensive."

Examinations of Professional and Technical Students. A

---

[1] *Laws of* 1877, c. 425.

[2] *Reports of the Examination Department,* iv, 102.

rule of the Court of Appeals adopted in 1882 required that all persons before entering upon a clerkship or substituted course of study for admission to the New York bar, if not a college graduate must pass certain of the Regents' academic examinations. In 1889, a similar requirement was exacted by statute [1] of all candidates for the degree of doctor of medicine; in 1894 every dental school in the State voluntarily adopted the Regents' academic credentials as the requirement for admission, and a year later the same preliminary education standard required in medicine was provided by statute for all dental and veterinary students. [2]

To meet these requirements the Regents have provided special examinations in academic subjects for those professional students who are not college graduates, and who have not already received the Regents' certificate of graduation from an academy or high school. These add somewhat to the examination work of the University, but they constitute a much less important share of the work than the regular academic examinations. In 1896 the total number of papers in the preliminary examinations for professional students was 23,000, and 1100 certificates were granted on the examinations. The significance of these preliminary tests is in setting a minimum standard of general education—the full high school course—for professional students.

A further development of the Regents' examination system has been in providing examinations in medicine, law, and for public accountants. Provision was made for medical examinations as early as 1872,[3] but as graduates of registered medical colleges were allowed to practice, there were almost no candidates for the Regents' examinations. In 1890, however, the University was made the only authority which

---

[1] *Laws of* 1889, c. 468.   [2] *Laws of* 1895; c. 626, c. 860.

[3] *Laws of* 1872, c. 746.

could issue licenses entitling doctors of medicine to practice
in New York.[1] At the same time, three boards of Medical
Examiners—one for each school of medicine—were created.
The members of these boards are appointed by the Regents
from nominations made by the State Associations of practi-
tioners. The Regents provide the examinations, each board
examines and marks the papers of the candidates belonging
to its school, and on the reports of these examiners the
licenses to practice are issued by the Regents.[2] In 1895
similar boards of Dental Examiners and Veterinary Medical
Examiners were established, which are appointed in the same
way and perform similar functions as the boards of Medical
Examiners.[3] The State Board of Pharmacy, created in
1884, and appointed by the Governor, examines candidates
in pharmacy and grants licenses independently of the
Regents.[4]

The examinations in law are held directly by the Regents,
who confer on successful candidates the degree of LL. B.
In two charters granted to new law schools in 1891, the
Regents reserved to themselves the degree-conferring power;[5]
and in the following year they held examinations for the
law degree.[6] These examinations have been held annually
since that time; the average number of candidates has
been about 150, and the number of degrees granted about
125.[7] The Regents' degree has the same position as those
granted by private institutions, and holders of it to secure
admission to the bar must also pass the examinations conducted by the Court of Appeals.

In 1896, the Regents were required to provide examinations for public accountants, and to issue credentials to

[1] *Laws of* 1890, c. 500.   [2] *Laws of* 1890, c. 507.
[3] *Laws of* 1895, c. 626, c. 860. [4] *Laws of* 1884, c. 361; *Laws of* 1885, c. 360.
[5] *Reports of Regents*, vol. 105, p. 70. [6] *Reports of Regents*, vol. 106, p. 70.
[7] *Reports of Examination Department*, iv., 34.

persons who had passed the tests, giving them the title certified public accountant. A board of examiners composed
of experts has accordingly been appointed by the Regents,
and the system of public accountant examinations inaugurated.

University Extension. By the University Law of 1889,
the field of the Regents was extended to include the charter-
ing of libraries, museums, summer schools, correspondence
schools, permanent lecture courses, and all other institutions
for promoting higher education. On the basis of these
powers, and under the leadership of Melvil Dewey,[1] the
Secretary of the University, a large and far-reaching plan of
university extension was formed. On the application of the
Regents, the legislature in 1891 appropriated $10,000[2] for
this work, and the machinery for the extension of university
teaching was at once put in operation. In this work the
Regents occupy the same position as they do in relation to
secondary education. They stimulate and supervise local
action, but the immediate and direct management is in all
cases under some local organization.

The work of the Regents' extension department is in four
divisions—public libraries, extension teaching, summer
schools, and study clubs. There are now about 150 local
libraries chartered by the University, and subject to the inspection of its officers. The University, in addition, has
nearly five hundred traveling libraries, which are loaned to
villages for a brief period on the petition of taxpayers. The
frequent result of the loan of one of these traveling libraries
is the establishment of a local public library. Extension
teaching has for its object instruction by lectures and classes,
with oral and written exercises for those who cannot utilize

---

[1] See address by Mr. Dewey at the 27th Annual Convocation, on *The Extension
of the University of the State of New York.* Conv. Proc., 1889, p. 73.

[2] *Laws of* 1891, c. 303.

regular teaching institutions.[1] The University has a list of lecturers who may be engaged for different courses, and Regents' examinations and certificates are provided at the completion of a course. This division is as yet less important than the public libraries work; in 1895, 29 courses were offered at 21 local centers, with a total attendance of 37,600.[2] In reference to summer schools, the chief work of the University has been the preparation of an annual bulletin containing a brief account of the courses, work and situation of the various schools in this country. Traveling libraries are loaned to these schools in New York State, and Regents' examinations and certificates are also provided. Study clubs are associations for home study, which may be organized in villages unable to employ a lecturer and maintain an extension course. Syllabuses of different courses of study prepared by the University can be used by such clubs, and further assistance is offered in guiding their reading and in placing at their disposal books, apparatus, traveling libraries, and exchanges.[3] In 1896 there were 122 of these clubs registered with the Regents, an increase of 52 over the previous year; 88 of these clubs had borrowed traveling libraries.

Administrative Organization. The board of Regents of the University now consists of the Governor, Lieutenant Governor, Secretary of State and Superintendent of Public Instruction *ex-officiis*, and nineteen members elected for life by the legislature. No salary is attached to the position. From its constitution the board is necessarily a slowly changing body, and this with the character of the members chosen places it above the distractions of political issues. The full board meets several times each year, but it is also

---

[1] *Reports of the Regents*, vol. 109, p. 89.

[2] *Extension Department Reports*, III, 346.

[3] *Reports of the Regents*, vol. 108, p. 119.

divided into seven committees, changed every two years, each of which has special charge of some department of the University's work. The Regents choose a Chancellor and a Vice-Chancellor from among their own number; they also elect a Secretary, who is a salaried officer and the executive head of the administrative details. Under the Secretary, who is also director of the State Library, is a large force of clerks, assistants and professional experts busied with the operation of the State Library and State Museum, the supervision of extension work, the marking of examination papers and the inspection of schools. The State Boards of Medical, Dental and Veterinary Examiners, and the Board of Examiners for certified public accountants are also part of the University organization. Finally there are four councils, representing the convocation on higher education, the colleges, the academy principals and the libraries, which are composed of five members each, appointed by the Chancellor of the University, one councillor each year to serve for five years. These councils are advisory bodies with which the Regents may consult on the interests of the institutions represented by them.

Unification of the State Educational Bureaus.—The explanation of the existence of two separate and independent State bureaus of education is to be found in historical conditions which are now outgrown. The academies and colleges which came under the supervision of the Regents of the University during the first half of the century all had their origin in voluntary private action; they were mainly supported by private endowments and tuition fees, and the amount of State aid given was small. These institutions were therefore considered as having only a quasi-public character, and the supervision exercised by the Regents was of a very unobtrusive character. On the other hand, the common schools, when established, were from the first intended as a system of public education, supported mainly, and eventually altogether, by public taxation, and receiving a large share of the necessary funds directly from the State. For these public schools, receiving large State grants, and intended to provide a minimum of education for every child in the State, an elaborate organization and a thorough central control were considered necessary. This work was entirely different in character from the supervision then performed by the Regents, and the enormously greater number of common schools as compared with the number of academies placed the task beyond the powers of the Regents under their existing methods. Therefore, although the Regents had been active in securing the establishment of the common schools, a distinct and independent authority was established to direct and control the new system.

To-day, however, these conditions have entirely changed. The secondary schools are no longer only quasi-public; they are, to almost the same extent as the common schools, supported by public taxation, and part of the local public school systems. Even more important than this change in the character of the schools has been the change in the methods of supervision exercised by the Regents. They are now simply a board of directors, governing an elaborate organization of administrative subordinates, who perform the work of supervision. The system of inspection and the extensive scheme of examinations exercise a more thorough control over the curriculum and the character of the instruction in the academies than is exercised by the Superintendent of Public Instruction over these features in the common schools.

In view of the fact that the secondary schools are now for the most part public schools, and that they are subject to an even stricter central control than the common schools, a unification of the dual central organization would seem to offer certain advantages. It would get rid of a perplexing and unnecessary complexity in the State administrative system, and possibly some saving in the expenses of central management could be made. Even more important gains from a union of this sort would come from the centralization of the experience of both departments, so that the methods which were found successful in one might be readily adopted in the other. Still further, if the consolidation were established on the wisest basis, the entire educational system might be placed wholly beyond the domain of partisan politics. With the spoils system eliminated, and educational officers selected entirely on grounds of competency, large improvements in the methods and results of public education could be expected.

Propositions for the unification of the dual educational system came before the Committee on Education of the Constitutional Convention of 1894; and on the abstract principle that unification would be advantageous to all concerned the committee was unanimous. Three different methods of bringing about the desired result were suggested:—

1. To make the Superintendent of Public Instruction elective by the Regents of the University.

2. To create a new central authority uniting in itself the functions of the University and the Department of Public Instruction.

3. To subordinate the University to the Department of Public Instruction.

The third of these plans was not seriously considered by the committee. The practice of the legislature in electing the Superintendent of Public Instruction on party grounds made it obvious that this method would only increase the influence of party politics upon the educational interests of the State. It was similarly felt that if a new central authority was created, it was highly probable that partisan considerations would have a predominating influence in the selection of the officers. On the other hand, the record and traditions of the Regents were a guarantee that their selections would be based solely on grounds of tested competence and the public interest.

The discussion of these methods brought out wide differences of opinion in the committee, especially on the fundamental question as to whether it was advisable to determine the matter by constitutional provision.[1] Accordingly the new constitution contains no provision for unification. It does however recognize the Regents of the University,[2] and so makes it impossible for the legislature by any plan of consolidation to abolish that body. Unification can therefore come only by transferring the State supervision of the common school system to the Regents.

[1] *Report of the Committee on Education*, in *Reports of the Regents*, vol. 108, p. 52.

[2] *Constitution of 1894*, art. ix, 2.

CHAPTER III

CHARITIES AND CORRECTION

1. *Historical Development of Charity Administration*

THROUGHOUT the colonial period the administration of public relief to the poor in New York was localized in the hands of town officers.[1] Legislation established rules of settlement, ordered the removal of vagrants and authorized the local rates;[2] but the assessment and collection of the rates was made by the town assessors and constables, and the distribution of relief was managed by the town overseers. The tax levy, however, had to be made by the supervisors as part of the county rate, the receipts were turned over by the town constable to the county treasurer, and then paid out to the local overseers.[3]

This was the general system; but there are also some exceptional provisions suggestive of the later development of county in place of town administration. The amendments to the Duke of York's Laws issued Oct. 30, 1665, contain a provision:[4] "That in regard the conditions of distracted persons may be both very chargeable and troublesome, and

---

[1] See J. Cummings, *Poor Laws of Massachusetts and New York*, for steps in the development of taxation to supplement the earlier system of voluntary relief. He does not, however, note that the Duke of York's Laws (1665) provided for the election of town overseers of the poor. Probably, too, the English settlements on Long Island had levied poor rates even before 1665.

[2] *Colonial Laws of New York*, 1683, c. 9; *Ibid.*, 1691, c. 6.

[3] This county supervision was established in 1691; in 1775 (c. 63) it was repealed for Ulster and Dutchess counties.

[4] *Colonial Laws of New York*, p. 79.

so will prove too greate a Burthen for one Toune alone
to beare, each Toune in the Rideing[1] where such person or
persons shall happen to bee, are to Contribute towards the
Charge which may arise upon such occasions." The laws
passed by the Assembly in 1691 and afterwards contain no
reference to this, and probably the entire problem of relief
of insane, as well as other poor, was left to the towns.

Another exception was established by a law of 1740,[2]
which provided that in Dutchess county the supervisors
should pay from the county treasury for the expense of in-
quests and burials of persons dying without estate, and for
assistance to persons "in real need of relief." The last provision evidently was intended, like the Massachusetts law of
1659,[3] to furnish aid to those without a settlement in any
town. Like all New York province laws, this had to be re-
enacted from time to time to keep it in force, and when the
enactment of 1760 expired in 1770 the law was not renewed.
Later legislation, however, shows that, without any legislative
authority, some counties recognized and supported a special
class of county poor besides the settled town paupers.

In the decade following the battle of Saratoga, three laws
on settlement and poor relief, passed by the State Assembly,
make some changes in administrative methods. By the law
of 1780[4] the county became more prominent. The supervisors not only levied the poor rate as part of the county tax,
but also determined the amount of this tax for each town.
But each town continued to pay for its own poor, and instead of the former roundabout method, the tax was to be
paid by the collectors directly to the town overseers, while

---

[1] Yorkshire, which included Long Island and Staten Island and the settled
country north of the Harlem river, had been sub-divided into three administrative
districts known as Ridings, *cf.* Yorkshire in England.

[2] *Colonial Laws of New York*, c. 705.

[3] J. Cummings, *op. cit.*, p. 24.   [4] *Laws of* 1780, c. 68.

the accounts of the overseers were to be audited by two justices of the peace in the county. The important change made by the law of 1784[1] was to substitute public officers for church officers in the administration of relief in New York and several other counties. The Act of 1788 regulated in great detail the questions of settlement and immigration, and made some changes in administrative methods. In granting relief, the overseers were allowed to make only such allowances as were ordered by a justice of the peace; the erection of work-houses was authorized, and small towns might unite for the joint erection or purchase of such a house. The amount of the tax for poor relief was to be determined for each town by the annual town meeting instead of the supervisors; but where a class of county poor was recognized, the county might continue its aid from the county revenue for that class. This last provision indicates that town aid did not fully meet the situation, and the general tendency of these changes is toward a larger administrative unit.

In 1809, the class of county poor was recognized by statute.[2] The support of destitute, unsettled persons who on account of sickness could not be removed to their place of settlement, was made a charge on the counties. The aid was to be furnished by town overseers, their allowances being subject to the approval of the board of supervisors.[3]

It was not until the third decade of this century that the system of county administration supplanted the town system. The first active measure in this direction was the Act of 1820,[4] authorizing the supervisors of Rensselaer County to erect a house of industry to which judges might order applicants for relief and disorderly persons to be moved, and to which overseers might send children found begging. The

---

[1] *Laws of* 1784, c. 35.

[3] *Ibid.*, 1817, c. 177.

[2] *Ibid.*, 1809, c. 90.

[4] *Ibid.*, 1820, c. 51.

management of this house of industry was to be by superintendents appointed by the supervisors; and the expense
was to be a charge on the county, but assessed on the towns
in proportion to the cost of supporting the paupers from
each town.   Furthermore, no town could be made subject
to the act without its own consent.

Although referring specifically to one county, the powers
under this act could be exercised by the board of supervisors of any other county on a two-thirds vote.   The new
system of relief rapidly commended itself, and in 1824 an
act was passed providing for the erection of poor-houses in
18 counties, and authorizing the excepted counties to adopt
the act.   In the next few years special acts for over twenty
other counties had been passed; and before long, throughout the state, the system of county poor-houses [1] supple-
mented, in many places supplanted, the method of outdoor
relief in the various towns. [2]   In some counties the erection
of the county poor-house did away with the distinction between county and town poor, the county assuming all the
expenses without reference to the number of paupers from
the different towns. [3]   In other counties, each town bore the
expense of supporting its own inmates, the county maintaining the poor-house and the expense of supporting the
" county poor."   The management of the poor-houses was
in all cases under superintendents appointed annually by the
board of supervisors; and the provisions for committal were
similar to those for the Rensselaer county house of industry.

The same years in which occurred the transition from
town to county administration are also marked by the development of a definite policy of state aid for special classes

---

[1] *Cf.* Poor Law Unions in England, 1835.

[2] Outdoor relief might continue to be granted by overseers on written order of
a justice of the peace.   *Laws of* 1827, c. 99.

[3] *E. g.*, Warren County.   *Laws of* 1827, c. 197.

of poor not reached by the local relief arrangements. Even before this there had been some state action of this sort. Thus, by an act of 1778, state aid was furnished to the families of New York soldiers in the war of the Revolution.[1] At the beginning of the century the support of manumitted slaves was undertaken by the state, allowances being made to the local overseers; and isolated cases of state relief to particular individuals are also found. In the aggregate, however, these early instances of state charities are insignificant.

In one sense the entire state appropriation to the common school system, begun in 1812, can be classed as a state charity; but the question of public education presents other than problems of relief; its administration has always been on distinct principles, and for these reasons it has been considered in another chapter. But the provisions for the education of the deaf and dumb partake much more of the nature of philanthropy, and the state aid for this purpose first granted in 1819[2] marks the beginning of a rapid development of the policy of state support to special charitable institutions. The first grant to the New York institution for the instruction of the deaf and dumb was followed by others to the same institution, and in 1823 a similar grant was made to a second institution in central New York.[3] The Act of 1827[4] placed the New York city institution under the supervision of the superintendent of common schools, who was also authorized to appoint the state pupils for that institution.

A further development of state relief for special classes of dependents began with the establishment of a state lunatic asylum. Early legislation[5] had simply authorized the local

---

[1] *Laws of* 1778, c. 45.   [2] *Ibid.*, 1819, c. 238.

[3] *Ibid.*, 1821, c. 250; *ibid.*, 1822, c. 234; *ibid.*, 1823, c. 189.

[4] *Ibid.*, 1827, c. 97.   [5] *Ibid.*, *Laws of* 1788, c. 31; *ibid.*, 1827, c. 294.

authorities to prevent dangerous lunatics from running at large, and in most places the only measure taken in regard to the indigent insane was to send them to the poor-house or to the county jail. The expense of maintaining a lunatic asylum with competent medical assistance was too large to be undertaken by the counties; and it was evident that one or two large asylums for the state would have the great advantage of economy in management. Instead, however, of following the policy of grants to private institutions, as in the case of deaf mutes, the legislature decided to construct a state institution. Appropriations were made, beginning in 1836, and in 1843 the state lunatic asylum at Utica was opened.[1] The direction of this asylum was placed under the supervision of a board of nine managers, appointed by the Governor, which selected the superintendent and other resident officers, inspected the institution and reported to the legislature. The statute for the management of the asylum required all indigent lunatics not incurable to be sent to the state institution; but other provisions seem to limit this. It was provided that each county was entitled to send one patient violently insane and recently attacked, and also such further patients as the asylum might accommodate, in proportion to the insane population of the county. It is clear, in any case, that the asylum was intended chiefly for recent and curable cases of insanity, and incurable patients were left as before to private institutions or the local poor authorities.[2]

The two lines of state action indicated by the provisions for deaf mutes and for lunatics were followed in subsequent acts for other classes. In 1846[3] a state industrial school (House of Refuge for Juvenile Delinquents) was established

---

[1] *Laws of* 1836, c. 82; *ibid.*, 1839, c. 310; *ibid.*, 1840, c. 109; *ibid.*, 1842, c. 135.

[2] *Cf. Laws of* 1838, c. 218.   [3] *Laws of* 1846, c. 143.

at Rochester; in 1851[1] an asylum for idiots at Syracuse. In 1847 state appropriations were first made to private orphan asylums, and in 1851 similar grants were made to the New York Society for the Reformation of Juvenile Delinquents and to the New York Institution for the Blind.[2]

The middle years of the decade 1860–70 which, as has been seen, are marked by notable extensions of central authority in educational administration, also begin a new period of state activity in charity administration. In 1865, the Willard asylum for the chronic insane was authorized,[3] and two years later a third insane asylum and a State School for the Blind were undertaken.[4] But of greater importance than these extensions of the former policy, was the creation in 1867 of a central board to supervise and co-ordinate the public charities throughout the state. Before this time the county superintendent of poor had been required to make annual reports to the secretary of state[5] of the "name, age, sex and native county of every pauper" relieved during the year, "with such other information as the Secretary of State may direct." This however did not call for any control or supervision of the local officers. The Act of 1867 provided for a board of eight unsalaried commissioners of public charities, appointed by the Governor.[6] All charitable and correctional institutions receiving state aid, except prisons, were to be visited at least once in each year by some member of the state board; and all city and county poor-houses at least once in two years. The investigations were to include examination into the finances, the methods of instruction, government and management, and the condition of buildings and grounds.

[1] *Laws of* 1851, c. 502.

[2] *Ibid.*, 1847, c. 485; *ibid.*, 1848, c. 76; *ibid.*, 1851, c. 254; *ibid.*, 1864, c. 419.

[3] *Ibid.*, 1865, c. 342.   [4] *Ibid.*, 1866, c. 666; *ibid.*, 1867, c. 93, c. 320, c. 744.

[5] *Ibid.*, 1842, c. 214.   [6] *Ibid.*, 1867, c. 951.

Under this statute, the duties of the state board ended with the report to the legislature on its examinations, and no authority was granted to institute improvements or to control the management of the various institutions. The leading influence in creating the Board and in defining its powers and duties was simply the need of some agency to furnish disinterested and reliable information which would enable the legislature to distribute the state grants to public and private charities wisely and prudently. The need of any active control was not recognized as yet. Nevertheless, the creation of a state board, even with such limited powers, was important as the first step; and the information collected by this board served to show the need for further authority, and thus led to the establishment of a stronger central control.

The first important advances were made by the legislation of 1873.[1] A more effective inspection of lunatic asylums was made possible by providing for a salaried State Commissioner in Lunacy. The State Board of Charities—the cumbrous name given in 1867 being now reduced to this simpler form—continued, however, to have general powers of inspecting the lunatic asylums, as well as other charitable institutions; and in other directions its powers were increased. It was authorized to appoint county boards of visitors for the county poor-houses; its powers of visitation were extended to all private charitable institutions; and all institutions for the care of the insane were to be licensed by it. In addition, there was imposed on the State Board of Charities the administration of the new State Paupers Act, by which state relief was to be granted to paupers who had no claim through settlement on any county. Further authority was conferred on the State Board of Charities in

[1] *Laws of* 1870, c. 281; *ibid.*, 1871, c. 699, c. 713; *ibid.*, 1873, c. 571, c. 661.

1880, by charging it with the administration of the act for the return of alien paupers;[1] and in 1883, by requiring its consent to the incorporation of orphan asylums in the State.[2]

In the care of the insane, a more striking development has taken place, culminating recently in the complete centralization of the management of all public institutions for that purpose. The construction of new State hospitals and the enlargement of older institutions for the insane had continued; but in many counties the chronic insane remained in the hands of the local authorities, and even the State hospitals were considered in many quarters as local institutions. The managers or trustees of each institution selected by the Governor were usually residents of the immediate neighborhood, and in the absence of any strong control and uniform direction the belief had become common that the management of these asylums was purely of local concern.[3]

In 1889[4] the State Commissioner in Lunacy was replaced by a Commission in Lunacy of three persons, all salaried, with much larger powers of inspection and authority to make and enforce recommendations for the management of the various institutions. A year later[5] this Commission, the chairman of the State Board of Charities and the Comptroller were constituted a board to divide the State into asylum districts and to recommend the construction of additional buildings so as to accommodate all the indigent insane in State institutions. When that condition had been reached, it was announced in the statute that the expense of the care of the insane should cease to be a county charge and should be borne by the State, and that no insane persons should be permitted to remain in county care. New York, Monroe and Kings Counties were exempted from this act, but pro-

---

[1] *Laws of* 1880, c. 549.   [2] *Ibid.*, 1883, c. 446.
[3] *Reports of the State Commission in Lunacy*, ii, 12.
[4] *Laws of* 1889, c. 283.   [5] *Ibid.*, 1890, c. 126.

visions were made to include them in its application when desired by the authorities of those counties.

Monroe County in 1891 transferred its asylum property to the State as part of the State system; and in the same year the construction of additions to the State hospitals and the transfer of the 2200 insane in the county poor-houses was begun. On December 2, 1891,[1] the Commission in Lunacy certified that sufficient accommodations had been provided for all the public insane of the State (other than those in New York and Kings Counties); a special tax for the support of the insane was levied by the Legislature,[2] and on October 1, 1893, the policy of State support was inaugurated.

When the State thus assumed the entire expense of maintaining its dependent insane, the defects of the former method of expenditure, and the need of some central supervision and control of the moneys to be expended, became self-evident. Accordingly, by the Estimate Law of 1893, the managers of the state hospitals were required to submit each month detailed estimates of their expenses to the State Commission in Lunacy, and payments were authorized only for the amounts certified by the Commission as necessary for the use of each hospital. In 1894[3] the necessity for securing the approval of the State Commission in Lunacy was extended to include expenditures for extensions and improvements as well as for maintenance.

Supported wholly from state appropriations, with the expenditures and all details of the management and care of the inmates under the strict supervision of the State Commission, the policy of centralization in the care of the insane was now realized. With the transfer of the institutions of New York

---

[1] *Reports of the State Commission in Lunacy*, v. 7.

[2] *Laws of 1893*, c. 214.   [3] *Ibid.*,1894, c. 358.

and Kings counties to the State in 1895 and 1896,[1] the system of State care of the insane, begun in 1836, became finally completed.

There remains to be noted some legislation within the last few years, by which the central supervision and control over other charitable institutions and local officers have been strengthened in some degree. An Act of 1894[2] required state charitable institutions, other than insane hospitals, to submit to the Comptroller statements of estimated expenses similar to the estimates submitted by the insane hospitals to the Commission in Lunacy; and a year later the Comptroller was given a power of audit over these institutions.[3] The State constitution of 1894, by provisions for the State Board of Charities and the Commission in Lunacy, recognized those boards as permanent parts of the state administrative system. The jurisdiction of the Board of Charities was, however, diminished by removing from its scope of visitation the insane hospitals and the reformatories for adult males, these institutions being placed under the control of the Commission in Lunacy and the Commission of Prisons. With these exceptions all institutions of a charitable, eleemosynary, correctional or reformatory character were made subject to the visitation and inspection of the Board of Charities. Furthermore, payments by local authorities to institutions under private control may be made only for inmates admitted under rules established by the state board.

These constitutional extensions of authority have been more carefully defined by the Legislature in the revised statutes on State Charities and the Poor Law[4]. Under these measures and with the all-important appropriations the effective authority of the State Board of Charities has been

---

[1] *Laws of* 1895, c. 628; *ibid.*, 1896, c. 2.   [2] *Ibid.*, 1894, c. 654.

[3] *Ibid.*, 1895, c. 13.   [4] *Ibid.*, 1895, c. 771; *ibid.*, 1896, c. 546, c. 225.

very materially increased over all charitable institutions in the State—those maintained by private corporations and local government as well as those supported from the state treasury. In addition to the occasional visits made by the members of the State Board of Charities, a department of inspection has now been organized under an Inspector of Charities who with his subordinates is permanently employed in visiting and examining the various institutions. Rules for the reception and retention of inmates have also been adopted by the state board; and detailed reports are required from all institutions to the Inspector of Charities. It is made the duty of the state board to call the attention of local officers and managers to abuses, defects or evils in the management of any institution, and they may also issue orders directing the adoption of their recommendations. These orders must first be approved by a justice of the Supreme Court, and wilful disobedience to an order so approved is to be considered a misdemeanor. This power of enforcing its recommendations is as yet closely limited; but with the comprehensive and thorough investigation and scrutiny of the charitable institutions in the State provided for, the control and influence of the State Board of Charities over the charitable activities of the State are made much more effective than before. Its power is in fact much more far-reaching and authoritative than that possessed by any other State Board of Charities in the United States. [1]

The leading features of this development may be briefly summarized: The colonial system of town relief continued in the main undisturbed until the third decade of the present century, when there came a rapid transition to the county poor-house system. Beginning about the same time as this transition, there developed a considerable amount of state

---

[1] *Reports of the State Board of Charities*, xxix, 74 (1895).

aid to special classes—notably the violent insane and deaf mutes. In 1867 the creation of the State Board of Charities established a limited amount of central supervision over state, local and private institutions, which was increased by later legislation. In 1873 the State Commissioner in Lunacy was provided; in 1889 the State Commission in Lunacy was established and the policy of state care of all insane inaugurated—a policy which was finally realized early in the present decade. Finally, the constitution of 1894 and subsequent legislation have made some important additions to the authority of theState Board of Charities over local and private charitable institutions.

The system of public charities now existing in New York State presents a most complicated series of organizations. There are in the first place the state insane hospitals, under the general direction and control of the Commission in Lunacy,—a completely centralized system, distinctly separate from the other charities, and, therefore, best considered in a separate section. Besides the insane hospitals, there are about a score of other state institutions and institutions under private management but supported by the state, including asylums for the feeble-minded, epileptic, blind and deaf mutes, reformatories and homes for veteran soldiers and sailors. There are also 56 county, four town and six city almshouses[1] supported and managed by the local authorities; and nearly 500 private institutions,—mainly asylums for dependent children and aged persons and hospitals for the sick. All of these state, local and private institutions are under the general supervision of the State Board of Charities, which has also powers of direct administration in reference to state, alien and Indian paupers. A discussion of the authority of this board will therefore make clear the existing system of

[1] City almshouses in New York, Brooklyn, Kingston, Newburgh, Oswego, Poughkeepsie.

central control over the charitable activities in this state
other than the care of the insane.

2. *The State Insane Hospital System*

The system of state insane hospitals is now governed by
the consolidated Insanity Law of 1896,[1] which provides for
the management of the existing institutions for the care of
the insane, regulates the commitment, care and discharge of
patients, and defines the powers and duties of the State
Commission in Lunacy.

Local Management.—For each hospital a board of seven
managers[2] is appointed by the Governor, with the consent of
the Senate; the term is seven years, one member of each
board retiring each year.   These managers must be selected
from the hospital district in which their respective institutions are located, except that the managers of the two
homeopathic hospitals may be appointed from any part of
the State.   The boards of managers establish rules and
regulations for the internal government and management of
their respective hospitals, and must maintain an effective
inspection of the same, making regular visits for that purpose.   Annual reports of their proceedings and the results
of their inspections must be made to the State Commission
in Lunacy, instead of to the legislature as formerly.   As
often as a vacancy occurs, each board of managers is empowered to appoint, subject to civil service rules, a superintendent, who must be a physician, a graduate of an incorporated
medical college, and of at least five years actual experience
in an institution for the insane.   The only other officer
appointed by the boards of managers is the treasurer.   A
majority of the board may remove the superintendent or
treasurer for cause stated in writing and after an opportunity
to be heard.

[1] *Laws of* 1896, c. 545.
[2] The Middletown Homeopathic Hospital has 13 managers.

The superintendent is the chief executive officer of the hospital, and, subject to the rules and regulations established by the managers, has full direction and control of the entire hospital and its equipment. He appoints, subject to civil service rules but without confirmation by the managers, all resident subordinate officers and employees, the number of each class being determined by the state commission. He may also remove any resident officer for cause stated in writing, after an opportunity to be heard, and may discharge any employé in his discretion. He must personally examine each patient within five days after admission, regularly visit all the wards or apartments for patients, and supervise a training school for nurses and attendants. Superintendents or their representatives are required to meet the State Commission in Lunacy in monthly conferences at Albany to consider the hospital estimates and other matters relating to the care and maintenance of the hospitals.

Commitment to any institution for the insane can be ordered only by a judge of a court of record, upon a verified petition and a certificate of lunacy signed by two qualified examiners in lunacy. Appeal may be taken within ten days from any such order to any justice of the Supreme Court, who must cause a jury to be summoned to try the question of insanity.

The State Commission in Lunacy, which has general supervision of the custody, care and treatment of the insane, consists of three commissioners appointed by the governor with the consent of the senate, for terms of six years, one member retiring every second year. The president of the commission must be a graduate of an incorporated medical college, having at least ten years' experience in the practice of his profession and five years' experience in the care and treatment of the insane; the second commissioner must be an attorney and counselor at law of not less than ten years' standing; and the third commissioner may be any reputable citizen. The salaries of the commissioners in the order named are $7500, $5000 and $3500, but the amounts are subject to change by the Governor, Secretary of State and Comptroller. In lieu of traveling expenses, an annual payment of $1200 is made to each commissioner.

The authority of the commission and its power of control over the administration of the Insanity Law, may be considered under three divisions: (1) Visitation, inspection and recommendation. (2) Adoption of regulations and forms. (3) Approval of estimates for expenditures.

The power of visitation and inspection extends to both state and private institutions for the care of the insane, and every institution must be visited at least twice in each calendar year by a majority of the commission, besides visits by individual commissioners. The power of inspection requires the commission to examine into the methods of management, the condition of buildings and grounds, the books and records, stores and food supplies, and the general and special dietaries; also to grant private interviews to patients, to inquire into complaints and to determine the fitness of officers and employees for their respective duties. The commission is further authorized to make such recommendations respecting the management or improvement of the institutions as it may, after such inspections, find necessary and desirable. The authority to examine and inspect thus granted is ample and complete; and although the direct power to enforce recommendations is not specifically given, enforcement can usually be secured through the other powers of the commission.

The commission has somewhat larger powers over the books of record and blank forms for official use in the hospitals. These must be uniform for all hospitals, and be approved by the State commission. The commission is

also required to make regulations in regard to the corres
pondence of the insane in custody, but cannot place restrictions on correspondence of any patients with the county
judge and district attorney of the county from which they
were committed.

A more effective control over the State hospitals is exercised by the provisions of the Estimate Law. By this
statute the superintendent of each State hospital must submit to the State commission monthly estimates " in minute
detail of the expenses required for the hospital of which he
is superintendent for the ensuing month." The commission
has full authority to revise these estimates as to quantity,
quality or estimated cost; and only after the revision and
approval of the commission is the Comptroller authorized
to issue warrants for the expenses of the hospitals.

The system of State care of the insane now established by
repeated acts of the Legislature and fixed in the permanent
policy of the State, is the most complete and comprehensive
which has ever obtained at any time or place. In no other
State or country as yet are all the dependent insane, whether
acute or chronic, maintained in State hospitals under one
administrative system and out of the proceeds of State
taxation.

Results of Centralization. The assumption by the State of
the care and relief of all the poor and indigent insane was
due to the proven deficiencies of the system of county care.
The investigations by Miss Dix in 1844, by a Senate Committee in 1857,[1] and by Dr. Willard in 1865, all demonstrated the deplorable condition of the insane in the county
poor-houses. The examination by the State Board of Charities in 1868 showed that in the county poor-houses there
were no attempts at classification; only in a few counties

---

[1] *Reports of the State Board of Charities*, xi, 25.

were regular attendants employed or medical attendance given; and the cells where violent cases were confined were usually dark, ill-ventilated and loathsome. After the opening of the Willard Asylum, the law provided that all chronic as well as acute insane be sent to State asylums, except in counties to which the State Board of Charities should grant exemptions. Owing to the inadequate accommodations in the State asylums, many counties continued to retain their insane; in some the regulations established by the Board of Charities before granting exemptions secured improvements, but many insane were kept by counties to which no exemption had been granted. In 1879,[1] of 1902 chronic insane in the counties, 818 were in counties with no proper accommodations for their treatment and care.

The fundamental difficulty with the system of county care was the high per capita expense of properly caring for the small number of insane in all but a few counties.[2] In large state institutions on the other hand administrative expenses become proportionately lower, saving may be made by purchasing supplies in large quantities, a proper classification of patients according to condition is possible, and better medical attention can be furnished. It is in these directions that direct state care of the insane has proved its advantages over the decentralized county method.

The State Commission in Lunacy has claimed that under state care " a higher recovery rate than before has been attained, while at the same time the death rate has been lower. . . . due no doubt, to the higher standard of care and treatment maintained under the State Care Act."[3] Statistical tests on this point are extremely difficult to make. As the state commission shows, it is unfair to compare the

---

[1] *Reports of the State Board of Charities*, xii, 52.   [2] *Ibid.*, xiv, 18.

[3] *Reports of the State Commission in Lunacy*, viii, 82; vii, 120.

present and former recovery rates of patients, in the state hospitals, since with the transfer of the chronic and incurable cases from the county asylums a reduction in recovery rate was to be expected. On the other hand the commission seems to deny the fact that such reduction in the recovery rate in the hospitals has taken place. They publish tables showing an increased rate by comparing the number of recoveries in the hospitals with the total number of insane in the state, holding that "of course there were no real recoveries in the poor houses."[1] This assumption of the commission can hardly be fully admitted. In the year 1871, forty recoveries were reported from the 1319 insane persons in the county poor houses, and even a very small proportion of recoveries in the counties would cause the increase shown by the commission to disappear. In the absence of any accurate record of recoveries from the county poor houses, there would seem to be no way of comparing accurately the statistics before 1889 with those subsequent to that year. Noting the figures since the county insane have been transferred, the few years thus far elapsed are scarcely sufficient to show general tendencies, as the results of these years are not uniformly in either direction. As yet the *a priori* belief that experienced physicians, trained attendants, classification of patients and specialized treatment will cause more recoveries and fewer deaths can not be substantiated by statistical results. It must be evident however that the recovery rate is not to be benefited by employing inexperienced physicians or cheap attendants and nurses unskilled in this special line of duty.

The results of the greater centralization of the financial administration under the Estimate Law can be more forcibly shown. For some time after the introduction of

---

[1] *Reports of the State Commission in Lunacy*, vi, 69.

the new system there was some friction and controversy
between the superintendents, managers and the state commission; but this has now disappeared, and substantial
accord and harmony rule.[1]　The effects of the new system
are shown by the reduction, during the first year of its operation, in the average cost of maintenance of over $30 per
capita,[2] while the standard of care has not been lowered, but
in various particulars has been raised.　The higher cost
under the former system of independent local administration
seems to have resulted mostly from lack of examination and
comparison with prices paid in other institutions.　The
comparisons instituted through the estimate system secured
immediately the large saving in annual expenditure already
indicated.[3]

3. *The State Board of Charities*

The general supervision of all charitable and benevolent
activities in the State other than the care of the insane is
under the direction of the State Board of Charities.　This
board consists of one commissioner from each of the eight
judicial departments of the State, one additional commissioner from the county of Kings, and two additional commissioners from the county of New York, all appointed by
the Governor, by and with the advice and consent of the
Senate, for a term of eight years.　The commissioners must
be residents of the respective districts from which they are
appointed, and no trustee or other administrative officer of
any institution, subject to the visitation of the state board,
may act as a member of the board.　No salary is allowed
the commissioners, but their expenses in the discharge of

---

[1] *Reports of the State Commission in Lunacy*, vii, 12–15.

[2] Per capita cost: 1892–3, $216.12; 1893–4, $184.84; 1895–6, $186.16.

[3] *Reports of the State Commission in Lunacy*, viii, 116.

their duties are paid by the State, and they may also receive ten dollars a day for each day's attendance at meetings.[1]

The board elects a president and vice-president from its own members; appoints a secretary, and such other officers and inspectors and clerks as it deems necessary, who hold office during the pleasure of the board. The principal additional officers now appointed are a Superintendent of State and Alien Poor, and an Inspector of Charities. A series of committees, at present numbering fifteen, are also appointed for different phases of the work of the board, and most of the active work of the board, outside of that done through its permanent salaried officers, is done through these committees or by individual investigations. The board, as a whole, holds from six to eight meetings a year, at which reports of work done are read, and plans and measures for future action are formulated and adopted.

The State Board of Charities has occupied a noteworthy position among the New York State administrative departments for the permanency of its tenure and the absence of all partisan influences in appointments. During the thirty years since the organization of the board there have been ten changes in the chief executive of the state, and several changes of political control, yet the only changes in the personnel of the board have been those effected by death or voluntary resignation. "The members who have been willing to continue in the service have been, without exception, re-appointed on the expiration of their terms."[2] One member of the original board remained in office 28 years; another member served 23 years; and eight others have served from 12 to 19 years. The same permanency of tenure is seen in the officers of the board. The first secretary, Mr.

[1] Under a provision in the Constitution requiring compensation to all State officers named therein.

[2] *Reports of the State Board of Charities,* xxviii, 14.

Charles S. Hoyt, held the position from 1867 until in 1895
he was made Superintendent of State and Alien Poor; and
Mr. J. O. Fanning, appointed assistant secretary in 1873,
likewise remained in that position until appointed Inspector
of Charities.

The activities of the State Board of Charities divide themselves easily into functions of supervision and functions of
administration. The latter includes the care, support and
removal of state and alien poor, and the support of Indian
poor persons; the former, the inspection and central control
of all state charitable institutions other than insane hospitals,
of private orphan asylums, hospitals and dispensaries, and
of the various county, town and city almshouses. These
powers of central supervision, the most inclusive, and the
most important for the purpose of this study, will be given
first attention, and the direct powers of administration considered later.

Supervision and Control. In this study of the authority of
the State Board of Charities over the state, local and private
institutions, it is important to distinguish the earlier position
of the Board and the results accomplished from the present
status under the legislation of 1895 and 1896. The first
problem is then to review the authority and work of the
board during the period from 1867 to 1895.

The duties of the State Board of Charities during this
period remained mainly visitorial, and its powers chiefly
advisory.[1] It had almost no power of control over the institutions and no authority to correct abuses. The responsibility for the management of the various institutions remained
wholly with the local authorities—whether trustees appointed
by the Governor, private corporations or local officials.
" It would appear that the Legislature in the creation of the

---

[1] *Reports of the State Board of Charities,* xx, 11.

board simply designed an agency by means of which it was to obtain information respecting the charities of the State. . . . The board constitutes the eyes of the legislature, and when it has visited and inspected an institution and made report thereon, it has exhausted its legal powers and performed to the fullest extent its legal duties," [1]

The weakness of its legal authority may be seen in its specific powers other than those of examination and report. Under the law of 1867, all applications from charitable institutions for state aid for *other than the usual expenses of management*, were required to be presented to the state board and to secure its recommendation before submission to the legislature. This guarded against extravagant appropriations for extensions and improvements, but made no provision for controlling the current management; and in practice did not always prevent extraordinary expenditures which the State Board of Charities opposed. [2] It was not until 1875 that a uniform system of records could be required of keepers of almshouses, [3] and not until four years later that the uniform system was extended to the State institutions. Since 1883 [4] the incorporation of orphan asylums must secure the approval of the State Board, but this again confers no power of control after the institution has been incorporated and opened.

Fortunately, however, the legal authority of the State Board of Charities does not adequately represent its work, measure the extent of its influence or the methods by which that influence is exerted. The state board has been ably reinforced in the work of visiting local institutions by volun-

---

[1] *Reports of the State Board of Charities*, xxviii, 10.

[2] The St. Lawrence Hospital for the Insane was constructed at an expense of $2500 for each inmate, against the strong protest of the State Board of Charities. *Reports of the State Board of Charities*, xxiii, 33.

[3] *Laws of* 1875, c. 140.   [4] *Ibid.*, 1883, c. 446.

tary committees in many counties;[1] which have been organized into the State Charities Aid Association. These local
organizations can make visits much more frequently than the
state board itself, and have been of much assistance in making public the condition of local institutions. The state
board has also succeeded in gaining the confidence and co-
operation of local officers and of the benevolent people engaged in the administration of public and private charities.[2]
In consequence, its recommendations and suggestions have
been kindly received and generally acted upon by the
county Superintendents of the Poor and the officers of the
various institutions. Since 1870 a state convention of
county Superintendents of the Poor has been held each
year, attended by from thirty to forty superintendents, by
supervisors from a considerable number of towns and by
members of the State Board of Charities, at which methods
of management and plans of improvement are discussed.
Through these means the state board has been enabled to
wield an influence far beyond its statutory powers, and to direct and control in some degree the charitable activities of
the state.

The results of this influence of the State Board of Charities are most strikingly exhibited in county poor relief and
in the state institutions. The first examination of the county
poor-houses, made in 1868, showed that in most cases their
management and condition were wholly inadequate and
unsatisfactory. The buildings were generally badly constructed and arranged, and many of them greatly out of
repair; a large proportion were without any adequate provision for the sick, and few of them were planned so as to
separate different classes of inmates. During the day the

[2] *Reports of the State Board of Charities*, vi, 10; xi, 9.

[1] *Laws of* 1873, c. 571. For regulations guiding these local visitors, see *Reports
of the State Board of Charities*, xv, 434.

aged, children, the sick, insane, epileptic, idiotic and blind, and the debased and able-bodied vagrant mingled freely.[1] An effort was made to separate the sexes at night, but owing to the defective character of the buildings even this could not in all cases be fully effected. Such conditions inevitably "served to sink the depraved still lower, and tended also to break down self-respect in the better class who, from sickness and other misfortunes, were compelled to seek public aid."[2]

The report of these conditions made by the state board to the legislature in 1869 attracted much attention, and soon led to great improvements in the buildings and also in the management of the county institutions. To aid in securing suitable buildings, the state board early prepared and published plans for the improvement and construction of almshouses, and furnished these to the local authorities.[3] During the next ten years new buildings with modern conveniences were erected in eighteen counties, and extensive improvements made in the poor-houses of twelve other counties.[4] In management, a stricter observance of the statutes regulating the transfer of the insane and feeble-minded to the appropriate state institutions, and a general improvement in the treatment and care of those remaining in county care, were early secured; and finally, as has been seen, the entire care of the former class was undertaken by the state. The idiotic and feeble-minded and epileptics are being transferred to State custody and care, as accommodations are provided. The State has now four institutions for these classes, which secure to them proper protection and care, impossible to be furnished in the poor-houses.

---

[1] Of 13,698 inmates, in 1868, there were found by actual count 2,261 children under 16 years of age, 3,111 insane, and 437 idiots. *Reports of the State Board of Charities*, xxx, 93.

[2] *Reports of the State Board of Charities*, x, 18.   [3] *Ibid.*, xi, 14.   [4] *Ibid.*, ix, 10.

Another notable improvement has been the removal of pauper children from poor-houses to asylums and family homes, where they may receive proper training and care instead of growing up with the associations of pauper life. From 1868 to 1874, the number of children in county poor-houses was reduced from 1222 to 593; and by 1894 there were only 134,[1] two-thirds of whom were under two years of age. In the city almshouses, little was done in this direction before 1875, when 1434 of the inmates were children; but in the next ten years this number was reduced to 650.[2] In 1896 there were less than 25 children over two years of age in county and city almshouses, except in New York and Brooklyn. These two cities, however, had over 1000 children over two years of age.[3] Furthermore, as a result of the examinations and recommendations of the state board, a more careful scrutiny regarding admissions to poor-houses came to be exercised by officials, and a better system of discipline enforced and maintained.

With these improvements in management the character of the county poor-houses has been changed. From being "the abodes of the able-bodied, idle and vagrant, as well as nurseries of pauperism and crime for children," they have become "largely homes for the aged and infirm, furnishing also comfortable accommodations for the enfeebled and sick."[4] The effects of greater watchfulness in admissions to the poor-houses are seen in the absence of any increase in the number supported in these institutions during the last thirty years. In 1868 the average number of persons supported in county and city almshouses was over 15,000; in 1896 it was under 14,000. Considering the growth of population, this showing is equivalent to a large decrease in the

[1] *Reports of the State Board of Charities*, viii, 18; xxviii, 560.

[2] *Ibid.*, xxviii, 563.   [3] *Ibid*, xxx, 482.   [4] *Ibid.*, x, 20.

proportion of paupers, even after making allowances for the pauper insane removed to the state insane hospitals. At the same time, a more careful and judicious expenditure, and a better system of accounting for public funds have made possible the improvements made with little or no increase in the total expenditure. In 1869 the county expenditure for poor relief was $1,330,000; in 1896 it was $1,515,000.

The various state institutions were not in any such deplorable condition as the county poor-houses at the time the State Board of Charities was created, hence the same sweeping and thorough-going reforms were not called for. But the board found opportunities here, also, to bring about many advantageous changes. In the case of the state insane hospitals its most important work was to induce the legislature to provide for extensions and new buildings to accommodate the insane; and it was due to its work that the state hospital system assumed proportions which made state care of the insane seem not altogether a revolutionary movement in administrative policy. In much the same way, the State Board of Charities has been influential in securing the extension of other State charities. Since 1867 there have been established two additional asylums for the feeble-minded, the Craig colony for epileptics, a home for veteran soldiers and sailors and three reformatories; and several other institutions are now in course of construction.

Improvements in the management of State institutions have been most needed in the case of reformatories, and under the supervision of the State Board of Charities the administration of these institutions has been placed on a much higher plane. It is only since this supervision was established that commitments to these institutions have been properly regulated,[1] and a system of classification es-

[1] *Reports of the State Board of Charities*, xxviii, 56.

tablished within them, leading to the abandonment of the
old prison theory and the adoption of true reformatory
ideas. The State Industrial School at Rochester illustrates
these changes: "For cells with iron-barred doors there
have been substituted open dormitories, and the space about
the buildings has been opened as grounds for play and exercise. . . . Physical culture and military drill have given
the boys a good carriage and manly bearing, while the
common and trade schools have given them occupation and
mental training which develops the best and represses the
worst characteristics."

Special investigations on charges of mismanagement and
cruelty in two reformatories will illustrate the methods of the
State Board of Charities, and how despite its lack of adequate authority, its work has been productive of good
results.

The investigation of the New York Juvenile Society was
important in securing a judicial decision upholding the right
of the State Board to conduct a summary inquiry without
specific charges, and without giving the defendant an opportunity to be heard by counsel or to cross-examine witnesses.[1]
The decision was based on the ground that such investigation
was a mere preliminary inquiry, which must be followed by
a judicial proceeding before action could be taken. The
result of the investigation showed that the society was in-
solvent, that the management of its affairs was such as to
discourage benevolence, and that it failed to fulfil the purposes of a charitable organization. With a report of these
facts and a request to the Attorney-General to institute proceedings in the courts, the authority of the State Board of
Charities ended; but the action having been brought, the

---

[1] N. Y. Juv. Guardian Soc. *v.* T. Roosevelt et al. Daly, C. J., in Court of Common
Pleas for City of N. Y. *Reports of the State Board of Charities,* xxviii, 71.

Supreme Court ordered that the corporate rights and franchises of the corporation be annulled and forfeited.

The Elmira Reformatory investigation[1] was a much more prominent case, and ended less satisfactorily. The charges against the managers of the Reformatory appeared first in the public press. The investigation by a committee of the state board lasted from September, 1893, to February, 1894, 25 sessions being held at Elmira, Albany, New York, Auburn and Clinton, and some 200 witnesses being examined. The report of the committee sustained many of the charges of cruelty against the general superintendent, and after an exhaustive discussion by the state board the report was adopted and submitted to the legislature. The legislature, however, took no action, and a special investigating commission appointed by the Governor reported, two in favor of the reformatory and one upholding the report of the state board. On this, the Governor dismissed the charges against the managers and re-appointed two whose terms had expired. The investigation by the State Board of Charities, however, secured some results. "Paddling" was at least suspended at the reformatory; an appropriation for $200,000 for an extension was defeated; and the passage of an act for an Eastern Reformatory was facilitated. On the other hand, the constitution of 1894 took the Elmira Reformatory from the supervision of the State Board of Charities and placed it under the Commission of Prisons, where, as an institution for adult criminals, it more properly belonged.

The constitution of 1894 and the statutes of 1895–1896 confer on the State Board of Charities a much wider scope of authority, and more effective control over the various institutions, than it possessed under its former powers of visitation and inspection. There is, in the first place, a new but

[1] *Reports of the State Board of Charities*, xxviii, 133.

vague requirement that the Board shall "maintain a general supervision" over the different institutions, "subject to its supervision by the constitution or by law." Of more importance are the provisions specifying, with considerable detail, the scope of the inquiries to be made on visits of inspection and the power of holding investigations, and making it the duty of the board to call the attention of local managers to abuses, defects or evils found in the institutions or in their administration. It is further provided that the board shall:

"Aid in securing the just, humane and economical administration of all institutions subject to its supervision."

"Advise the officers of such institutions in the performance of their official duties."

"Aid in securing the erection of suitable buildings for the accommodation of the inmates of such institutions."

"Aid in securing the best sanitary condition of the buildings and grounds of all such institutions, and advise measures for the protection and preservation of the health of the inmates."

"Aid in securing the establishment and maintenance of such industrial, educational and moral training in institutions having the care of children as is best suited to the needs of the inmates."[1]

These provisions, if lacking in definiteness and authority, will at least add moral strength to the recommendations of the board.

Some more definite powers are, however, conferred. No almshouse may in the future be built or reconstructed, in whole or in part, except on plans and designs approved in writing by the State Board of Charities. Further, the state board is required to establish rules for the reception and retention of inmates at institutions under private control but

[1] *Laws of* 1896, c. 546.

supported in part by counties, cities, towns or villages; and under the constitution payments may be made to such institutions only for inmates received in accordance with such rules.

These additional powers of supervision are made really effective by a brief clause of five words, which of itself would have added much to the authority of the state board. Where formerly official visits could be made only by the board or individual members, now "inspectors duly appointed by it" are equally authorized. The department of inspection established under this provision consists of a chief inspector and a number of subordinates, who give their whole time to this work, where formerly only such occasional visits as could be expected from a body of unsalaried officials were made. Obviously, the extent of this additional power of inspection depends, to a large degree, on the number of inspectors. For the first year five were employed,[1] but it was the intention of the board to increase the number when adequate funds were provided by the legislature to secure the services of skilled and discreet agents.

The work of these officials has thus far been principally directed to securing the enforcement of the rules adopted by the board for the reception and retention, at public charge, of inmates of private charitable institutions. About one-half of these private charities receive aid from local authorities. The institutions for the care of children, usually called orphan asylums, receive the largest amounts, and few of them could long survive the withdrawal of revenues from public sources.[2] They are so largely dependent on this that they might almost be classed as public institutions. Hospitals are not so largely supported from public funds, but

[1] *Reports of the State Board of Charities*, xxx, 102.
[2] *Ibid.*, xxix, 75.

modest appropriations are made to many by city and county authorities.[1] These expenditures from public sources have hitherto been subject to no supervision, even by local authorities. The rules established by the State board are intended to secure the removal to the care and custody of parents, relatives or friends, of those not legitimately dependent on public charity. Under the rules, an acceptance from the local officer of the poor is necessary before any person can be admitted as a public charge upon the locality he represents, and such acceptances must be renewed yearly to allow retention of inmates at public expense. The necessity of securing a certificate from the State board, of obedience to these rules, guards against improper admissions and unnecessary retentions.

The effect of these regulations was at once visible. During the first year there was a net decrease of 1248 in the number of inmates who were a public charge in the 120 institutions for the care of destitute and dependent children. In New York City, in order that the acceptances of the City Commissioners of Charities might be granted intelligently, six examiners have been appointed through the influence of the State board, and the results of the operation of the rules in that city for ten months, ending December 31, 1896, were the rejection of 3761 cases, and an estimated annual saving to the city of $450,000.[2]

In addition to the local inspections for the purpose of securing obedience to the rules of the State board, the department of inspection has charge of the reports and records required by the rules, including the collection, examination, correction and compilation of reports from 12 state institutions, 8 schools for the deaf, 60 almshouses, 287 orphan asylums and homes for the aged, 156 hospitals and

---

[1] *Reports of the State Board of Charities,* xx, 51.　　　[2] *Ibid.,* xxx, 103.

89 dispensaries. The most important and onerous work has been the compilation and classification of the monthly returns from the institutions for the care of children, so as to furnish an intelligent basis for the work of inspection already explained.

The work of the department of inspection has not resulted in any less active work by the members of the state board. Visitations and examinations by the individual commissioners in their respective districts, the regular and special investigations of institutions by committees of the board, and special examinations of methods and plans of charitable work are continued as before. The control exercised by the board through its power of approving the incorporation of private charitable organizations should be specially noted. Whenever any application for approval is made, it is referred to the commissioners of the district from which it is made,[1] who make a personal examination and inquiry into the merits of the application, especially as to the necessity for such an institution as is proposed, the character and standing of the proposed incorporators, and the financial resources of the association. On the detailed written report from the commissioner, the board takes action; and it has not hesitated to disapprove applications if it is not assured of the need for the organization, and of the prospect of satisfactory management. Thus, in 1894, of nine applications made, only five were approved. The control of the board is, however, deficient, owing to its lack of power to dissolve incorporations, and it has asked that such power be conferred on it, so as to provide a speedy way of closing unworthy and undesirable institutions.[2]

Direct Administration. Owing to the character of the State Board of Charities as a body of unsalaried officials,

---

[1] *Reports of the State Board of Charities,* xxviii, 69.   [2] *Ibid.,* xxx, 80.

the functions of direct administration imposed on it were
naturally performed by its secretary, and these duties occupied much the greater part of that officer's time.   In 1895
the position of Superintendent of State and Alien Poor was
established by the board, and Mr. Hoyt, who had served as
secretary since 1867, continued his old duties under the
new title.   These duties are the execution of the laws relating
to state, alien and Indian paupers.

The class of state paupers established in 1873 consisted
of those poor persons who had no established settlement in
any town.   The New York law by which one year's residence established a settlement made the unsettled poor a
much smaller class than in other States, and the problem of
their relief did not early become pressing.   But, as the
number increased with the growth of population, the county
authorities considered this class an unjust burden, and it
became the practice to send them from one county to another so as to avoid the expense of their maintenance and
care.[1]   It was estimated that $200,000 was spent annually
in thus shifting responsibility; while most of the persons
were in no way improved, and in time many of them became
so enfeebled that they could no longer be transported, and
had to be permanently provided for by some locality.

Under the State Paupers Act of 1873 such unsettled
paupers are furnished immediate relief at the expense of the
State in certain county poorhouses selected for the purpose
by the State Board of Charities.   Many being relieved without delay recover from temporary infirmity and are able in
a short while to provide for themselves.   The more important work of the Superintendent of State and Alien Poor,
however, consists in making inquiries to ascertain the legal
habitation of such persons, and in providing them with trans-

[1] *Reports of the State Board of Charities*, xii, 30.

portation to friends or their place of settlement, where they may be supported by those on whom the burden should fall.

Alien paupers differ from other State paupers only in that their homes being in Europe, transportation has to be furnished out of the country.

Of the 33,000 state paupers committed from 1873 to 1896, 8,900 have been discharged as self-supporting, 1,700 have absconded and disappeared, 760 have died, and 21,500 have been furnished transportation. The whole number of alien paupers removed to their homes since 1880 has been 2,860. The financial saving to the state from a single year's return of paupers, considering the cost of maintaining such paupers for the average duration of their lives, has been estimated at $2,500,000, and the total saving up to 1897 at $36,000,000. The execution of these laws has been conducted with such fidelity and painstaking care by the Superintendent that the Board of Charities " has yet to hear of a single criticism or complaint in regard to his conduct of the delicate and important duties intrusted to him."[1]

Indian paupers are supported in county poor-houses at state expense, but the number in this class is insignificant, and this work unimportant.

The Extent of Centralization. It will be evident from this study that the central administrative control over local officials in the administration of charities even under the recent legislation is much less extensive and authoritative than the control of the State Superintendent of Public Instruction over local school officials. The State Board of Charities has no authority corresponding to the appellate jurisdiction of that officer, and its direction of the local management is much narrower in its scope than his. On the other hand, a

[1] *Reports of the State Board of Charities*, xxx, 85–89.

great proportion of the public charities have been assumed entirely by the state, and the supervision of private charities is a state and not a local function. The extent of this centralization may be shown by comparing the $3,000,000 expenditures for local institutions, with the $7,000,000 expended by the state, and the $14,000,000 expended by private institutions under state control.[1] From this point of view, the public administration of charities is much more centralized than the administration of the common school system, or any other governmental function in which local action has been predominant.

But while as compared with the local authorities, the State charitable administration occupies a much larger field, the most striking characteristic of the system of poor relief in New York State, as in the United States generally, continues to be the extent of its private charities. "From the original settlement of the country until now, poor relief has been held to be primarily a duty, not of cities or States, but of neighbors, townsmen, churches and friends."[2] Not only the private institutions subject to State supervision, but also a vast number of voluntary philanthropic agencies, such as churches, missions, etc., are active in this work. In New York City there are nearly 2,000 such voluntary associations, and it is estimated that the amount expended for relief

---

[1] Public expenditures for charitable purposes in 1896:

County poor-houses	$1,515,138
City almshouses	1,649,071
Total, local institutions	$3,164,209
Insane hospitals	$5,254,908
Other State institutions	969,500
State reformatories	1,073,471
	$7,297,879

Of the $14,000,000 expended by private institutions, $3,000,000 is received from county and city funds.

[2] F. G. Peabody in *Charities Review*, vii, 930–935 (January, 1898).

through such sources in the State is equal to 50 per cent. of that furnished through public and private institutions. This expenditure is not subject to any direct government control and direction, but is organized so as to secure intelligence and security through the Charities Organization Society, another voluntary organization founded in 1882 through the initiative of the State Board of Charities.[1] The existence of this vast amount of private and voluntary relief must be borne in mind in any estimate of charity administration in New York State.

4. *The Administration and Supervision of Penal Institutions*

Under the Dutch governors of New Netherlands, Fort Amsterdam was used as the only prison in the colony, its management being part of the central government. But with the development of the colony, after the transfer to the English, there arose the need for jails or prisons in the outlying districts, and these were accordingly constructed under the direction of the justices of the peace, while the care and management of the prisoners was one of the functions of the sheriffs. The establishment of the supervisor system of county taxation[2] did not involve the transfer of prison management to the new officials, and until the middle of the eighteenth century the appointed justices of the peace continued, under special acts of the legislature, to levy taxes for repairs and the construction of new buildings.[3]

Beginning in 1741, the acts authorizing the levy of taxes for county jails and court-houses sometimes designate the supervisors in place of the justices;[4] but in other cases the

---

[1] *National Conference on Charities and Correction,* 1893, p. 59.

[2] See chap. v, 1.

[3] *Laws of* 1704, c. 144; *ibid.,* 1715, c. 300; *ibid.,* 1719, c. 373; *ibid.,* 1725, c. 505.

[4] *Ibid.,* 1741, c. 715; *ibid.,* 1745, c. 807; *ibid.,* 1751, c. 915; *ibid.,* 1760, c. 1115; *ibid.,* 1765, c. 1288; *ibid.,* 1768, c. 1349.

justices continued to be named,[1] and it is not until 1760 that the transition to independent local control of prison construction was fully accomplished. The management of county jails and the care of prisoners by the sheriffs remained longer under some central control. As we have seen, the sheriffs were appointed by the central government until the adoption of the constitution of 1821,[2] and it was not until then that jail management became completely localized.

Before that time, however, a centralized system of prison administration for certain classes of criminals had been established. In 1796 the construction of two state prisons at New York and Albany was provided for, and in 1815 another prison at Auburn was authorized. To these state prisons were sent all convicted felons or habitual criminals, and only the misdemeanants or less hardened and vicious cases were sentenced to confinement in county jails. A system of classification was thus established, and the care and management of the most important part of prison administration became a function of the state authorities.

The number of state prisons naturally increased with the growth of population. In 1825 the Sing Sing prison was authorized, and in 1844 that at Clinton. The New York and Albany institutions were, however, turned over to the local authorities to be used as county penitentiaries. The managers of the various state institutions were independent of each other and of all central supervision. In 1847 a board of Inspectors of Prisons, elected by popular vote, was created.[3] Their power at first included the visitation and examination of county jails, but in 1849 that part of the law was repealed.[4] Their authority over the state institutions included the power to visit and examine the prisons, to make regulations for their government and discipline, to prescribe

[1] *Laws of 1743*, c. 756; *ibid*, 1758, c. 1060.   [2] See p. 12.
[3] *Constitution of 1846; Laws of 1847*, c. 460.   [4] *Laws of 1849*, c. 331.

articles and quantities of food, and to appoint the officers. Instead of acting jointly, each inspector was given complete charge of a particular prison; and through this provision the management of each prison continued, as before, to be very largely independent.

This system of prison administration was continued for nearly thirty years. In 1876, however, as the result of an investigation into the condition of the State prisons by a legislative commission, the management of these State institutions was concentrated under a single officer. The report of the commission had shown that the prison officers were appointed mainly through political influence; that appointees were inefficient, discipline was lax, the prisons were much overcrowded and the convicts subjected to much abusive treatment.[1] The result of this report was the adoption of a constitutional amendment creating the office of Superintendent of Prisons. To this officer, who was appointed by the Governor, was given the management and control of all state prisons, including all matters relating to their government, discipline, police, contracts and fiscal concerns.[2] The wardens, physicians and chaplains were made appointees of the Superintendent, who had also the authority to remove any of them and to designate the number of subordinate officers.

The effects of the change in the system of prison administration were seen most strikingly in the fiscal statistics. In 1876, the deficit after deducting the earnings from prison industries was $605,040. In 1877, the expenditures were $625,000, and the deficit $317,000.[3] Under the new management, the expenditures were at once reduced by fifty per cent. and the earnings so increased that by 1879 the deficit was only $20,000, and by 1881 it had been changed

---

[1] *Report on Investigation of State Prisons*, 1876.   [2] *Laws of* 1877, c. 107.
[3] *Report of the Superintendent of Prisons*, iii, 3; xvi, 9.

to a surplus. The prisons continued to be self-supporting until 1887, when the agitation against the competition of prison-made goods with free labor led to legislative regulations which hampered the prison industries, and deficits again appeared.

In 1877 the State Reformatory at Elmira was opened, where, for the first time in America,[1] adult felons were committed on an indeterminate sentence, and treated under a system of progressive classification and conditional release based upon attainments in conduct and character while in prison. This institution was not placed under the State Superintendent of Prisons, but has an independent management, although, as we have seen, it was under the general supervision of the State Board of Charities until 1894.

While the management of the state prisons became completely centralized, changes of another character had been gradually made in other features of prison administration, through the development of the penitentiary system. When, in the counties where large cities grew up, the former jails became entirely inadequate for the large number of misdemeanants, the construction of new and larger institutions was authorized. These penitentiaries, which were built in six counties, at first contained the same class of prisoners as the county jails; but subsequent changes led to the concentration in these large institutions of all classes of prisoners, thus breaking down to a large extent the system of classification which the use of state prisons had inaugurated.

The first measures leading to this result were the laws authorizing the penitentiaries to receive prisoners from other counties. Many counties soon found it cheaper to board their prisoners at the large penitentiaries than in their own

[1] R. Brinkerhoff, *The Prison Question,* in *Report of the National Conference of Charities and Correction,* 1893, p. 149.

small jails; and the result was that the latter became very largely places for the detention of persons awaiting trial, while the great number of convicted misdemeanants were sent to the penitentiaries. The county magistrates further promoted this tendency by abandoning, in large measure, twenty, thirty and forty day sentences, punishing by fine those not sentenced for the sixty days necessary to secure admission to the penitentiaries.[1]

This concentration of misdemeanants at the penitentaries would not have been important but for other measures which have filled these institutions with grosser and more vicious felons. The penitentiary managers were authorized to receive prisoners from federal courts, both in and out of New York State; and in this way homicides, counterfeiters, stage-robbers and felons of various kinds were admitted. Still further, statutes were passed permitting the state courts to sentence to a penitentiary felons whose terms of imprisonment did not exceed five years. For the board and care of such felons the state paid the penitentiary authorities, although they could have been maintained at less expense at the state prisons, where the state would also have had the benefit of their labor.

It was about twenty years after the complete centralization of state prison management before any steps were taken toward any central control of the penitentiaries and county jails. The constitution of 1894 directed the legislature to provide a Commission of Prisons to "visit and inspect all institutions used for the detention of sane adults charged with or convicted of crime, or detained as witnesses or debtors." Under this provision, the legislature in 1895 provided for a commission of eight persons, to be appointed by the Governor, one from each judicial district, one member to retire each year.[2] The commissioners receive ten dollars

---

[1] *Reports of the State Commission of Prisons,* i, 21.   [2] *Laws of* 1895, c. 1026.

per day for time employed in attending the meetings of the commission; and the secretary, elected by the commission, receives a salary of $3,000 per year.

The functions of the State Commission of Prisons are in part administrative, in part supervisory. In the first class fall its duties in reference to the employment of convicts in the State prisons. The statute establishing the commission required it to prepare a Convict Labor Law, providing for the employment of prisoners in the manufacture of articles required by the State, or its political divisions. Such a law was prepared and enacted in 1896.[1] In the operation of this law the Commission assigns the industries to be performed in each of the State prisons; and, in conjunction with the Comptroller, the Superintendent of State Prisons, and the Commission in Lunacy, it fixes the prices to be charged for the articles made. The general management of the prison industries is under the direction of the State Superintendent of Prisons.

The new system has been in operation only a short time, and the financial results are as yet unfavorable. In 1897 the receipts from prison-made goods were less than the expenditures for these institutions by $560,000. It is hoped that after the new method has been in operation longer a better showing may be made; but in any case it has been demonstrated that the requisitions of state and local officers and institutions will be sufficient to provide productive employment for all the available convicts in the prisons.[2]

The supervisory powers of the Commission of Prisons resemble those of the State Board of Charities. It does not interfere with the detailed administration of the State Superintendent of Prisons; but it has general authority to visit and inspect the state prisons and reformatories, and also

---

[1] *Laws of* 1896, c. 429.

[2] *Reports of the Superintendent of State Prisons for 1897.*

the county jails and penitentiaries. This authority makes it their duty to investigate the management of all these institutions, and the conduct and efficiency of persons charged with their management; to aid in securing just, humane and economic administration; to secure the best sanitary condition of buildings and grounds; and to aid in securing the erection of suitable buildings. For this last purpose it is authorized to approve or reject plans for the construction or improvement of buildings. Further, it is to collect statistical information concerning the various institutions, for which purpose the wardens and keepers of the various institutions are required to make reports.

The visits and inspection of the local institutions by the commission have disclosed the importance of a central supervision of these institutions. In the penitentiaries the effects of the association of felons and misdemeanants was at once evident, and the commission has secured the passage of laws requiring all felons sentenced for a term exceeding one year to be sent to the state prisons or reformatories,[1] and prohibiting the reception of United States convicts in the penitentiaries.[2] These statutes will secure the separation of misdemeanants and felons, and thus establish a distinct differentiation of functions between the state and county institutions. The commission's inspections have also shown that in several penitentiaries there are a large number of convicts who are not kept employed;[3] while in forty-nine of the sixty counties the jail convicts are not employed in any form of labor at all.[4] The period of detention is thus rather a vacation than a punishment; and in idleness the young offenders listen to the stories of older criminals and receive lessons in criminal ways. The commission has attempted to

---

[1] *Laws of* 1896, c. 553.   [2] *Ibid.*, 1896, c. 429.

[3] *Reports of the State Commission of Prisons*, iii, 81.   [4] *Ibid.*, iii, 86.

secure a more general obedience to the law on this subject. It has especially advocated the employment of convict labor in building and improving highways; not only
as the best way of employing convicts without affecting
outside labor, but also as a means of securing well-built and
passable country roads.

The most serious defects in the county care of prisoners
were found in the condition of the county jail buildings.
" The great majority of the jails in this State are relics of
another generation, when the sole object was confinement,
and no consideration was given to the health or reformation
of the inmates."[1] One building now in use was constructed
in 1801, and ten are more than forty years old. Some of
these have had later additions and improvements, but
most of them, and many of those constructed later, have
insufficient accommodations for the number of inmates they
at times receive. Westchester county jail with 72 cells has
held 500 prisoners. Many jails have no system of separat-
ing different classes of inmates; and debtors, witnesses,
women and children are confined together. In Greene
county a boy 14 years old, charged with assault on a school-
mate, was in the same compartment with persons indicted for
murder and bigamy, and it was believed that when the
grand jury met in three months the boy would be acquitted.
Even where there was some classification it was frequently
inadequate for all purposes. Still more frequent were cases
of poor ventilation, poor drainage and bad sanitary conditions. More than half of the jails examined in 1896 were
defective in one or more of these respects, rendering them
sources of danger to the health not only of the inmates, but
also of the localities where they were situated.

The visiting commissioners called the attention of the

---

[1] *Reports of the State Commission of Prisons*, iii, 84.

county authorities to these defects, and recommended improvements. Five jails were in such condition that they were considered unfit for occupation and beyond hope of improvement by repairs; the only advice to be given in these cases was to tear down the old jail and erect a new building. The recommendations of the commissioners were in many counties favorably received by the supervisors.[1] The officials have shown a disposition to improve the cleanliness of the jails, and to act on suggestions for the separation of different classes of prisoners so far as practical with the buildings in use. In some cases more radical improvements were begun, and in two counties steps were taken to build new jails. The inspections of the commission have therefore done much good already; but as in all cases where the central body has only an advisory authority, improvements recommended by it come gradually, and the full results of the supervision of county jails by the Commission of Prisons can be tested only after a lapse of years.

There is, however, in the revised Prison Law of 1898, some extension of the authority of the commission. It is empowered to appoint salaried inspectors to visit penal institutions, thus making possible a more constant supervision of the local institutions. In making investigations it is authorized to issue subpœnas and examine persons under oath. It is *required* to make and enforce uniform rules and regulations for all county jails and penitentiaries in respect to the separation, labor, treatment and discipline of all prisoners confined therein. The commission is also given statutory authority to issue specific orders to the local officials in regard to the construction and management of county penal institutions; and provision is made for the enforcement of these orders. These directions may ask for a

[1] *Reports of the State Commission of Prisons*, ii, 28.

modification in the treatment of prisoners, or a change in the method of management; they may require the construction of new buildings or improvements, so as to provide adequate accommodations, separation of prisoners, ventilation, bathing facilities, or to remove any conditions which are liable to affect the health or morals of the prisoners.

If the directions of the commission are not followed, it may apply to a justice of the Supreme Court for an order requiring that the directions be obeyed. To secure these judicial orders, it will be necesssary to satisfy the judges that the improvements ordered by the commission are reasonable; and the commission's power of enforcement is, to this extent, limited. But with the increased scope of authority granted in the statute, and with the power of initiative to secure the judicial orders, the influence of the commission should be much enlarged, and its control over the county institutions should become more effective. Whether it prove an important advance or not, this latest legislation is at least an indication that the movement towards further central control is not losing ground.

CHAPTER IV

PUBLIC HEALTH ADMINISTRATION

1. *Historical Sketch of Health Legislation*

THE object of all but the latest public health legislation in New York State has been to guard against the danger from epidemic and contagious diseases. The first efforts were directed solely against the introduction of such diseases from abroad, and it is only within recent years that the importance of internal sanitary conditions on the health of the community has come to be recognized.

The early quarantine regulations were both issued and enforced by the central administrative authorities of the colony. As far back as 1647, we find the Council of New Netherlands taking measures to prevent the introduction of yellow fever, then prevailing in the West India Islands. In 1714 a quarantine was established at Staten Island by order of His Majesty's Council. In 1743 Governor George Clinton required all vessels coming to New York to be inspected and a health certificate issued before landing was allowed.[1]

Such executive orders continued to be the basis of quarantine rules until 1755, when the provincial assembly passed an act[2] forbidding all vessels having on board contagious distempers from approaching nearer the city of New York than Bedlow's island, and providing that a surgeon should be appointed by the governor to visit suspected vessels.

---

[1] Chadbourne and Moore, *Public Service of New York,* ii, 425, 446.

[2] *The Colonial Laws of New York,* c. 973.

124

In 1784[1] this law was substantially re-enacted by the state legislature, with the additional provision that in the absence of the Governor the execution of the act was to be under the direction of the mayor of New York City. Ten years later,[2] the scope of the act was extended to the whole of the State, the appointment of inspecting physicians at Albany and Hudson was authorized, and the mayors of these cities were empowered to enforce the law.[3] The powers thus vested in the mayors did not, however, constitute any great decentralization in the administration of the quarantine regulations, for the mayors were appointed by the Governor, and, what is more important, the real work of carrying out the law rested with the inspecting physicians or health officers appointed by the Governor.

Thus far the only means of internal sanitary regulations was through orders for the removal of nuisances, which, under the common law, could be issued by any justice of the peace. A yellow fever epidemic in the summer of 1795[4] roused the legislature to the need of more effective measures. By a statute of 1796,[5] a health officer and seven commissioners of the health office were to be appointed to enforce the quarantine regulations; and the need for internal regulation was recognized by authorizing the corporation of New York City to make rules for cleaning streets, and for the removal of offensive articles. The next year[6] the number of health commissioners was reduced to three, and the above powers of the city corporation were transferred to this board of state officials. A centralized system of sanitary regulation, as well as of quarantine, was thus established.

---

[1] *Laws of* 1784, c. 57.   [2] *Ibid.*, 1794, c. 53.

[3] Troy was added in 1827, c. 14.

[4] There were 525 deaths in New York City between July 19th and October 6th. *Memorial History of New York*, iii, 139.

[5] *Laws of* 1796, c. 38.   [6] *Ibid.*, 1797, c. 16.

In 1805 [1] a statute was enacted transferring the powers of the health commissioners to the mayor, aldermen and commonalty of the city of New York, who were authorized to establish a local board of health. [2] Quarantine remained as before under the control of the state officials, but internal sanitary regulations were now placed in charge of a local authority independent of any central control. The city of Albany received similar power in 1806 [3] to establish a local board of health; and in 1824 [4] the trustees of the village of Brooklyn were constituted a board of health.

Although these local boards of health dealt with internal sanitary conditions, their activities were confined to efforts to check the ravages of yellow fever, which in spite of quarantine regulations reappeared and became epidemic from time to time. As these epidemics were confined for the most part to the ports which had direct communication with the yellow fever regions in the West Indies, the interior towns found no need for special health authorities. Hence the small number of local boards in the first quarter of the century.

In 1832, however, the first visitation of Asiatic cholera to America forced on the legislature the temporary adoption of a more comprehensive scheme of local organizations for protection against that scourge. In New York City alone there were 2996 deaths, and whether due to the nature of the disease or to the increasing facility of transportation, there were victims of cholera in almost every considerable town in the state. [5]

The Act passed by the legislature of New York in this emergency provided that:

[1] *Laws of* 1805, c. 31.

[2] The creation of a local board was made mandatory by Act of 1820, c. 229.

[3] *Laws of* 1806, c. 109.   [4] *Ibid.*, 1824, c. 201.

[5] D. Atkins, editor, *Report on the Epidemic of Cholera* (1832).

"It shall be the duty of the common council of every city, and the trustees of every incorporated village in the several counties of this State bounded by Lakes Erie, Ontario and Champlain or on the rivers St. Lawrence or Hudson, or bounded on or intersected by any of the canals of this state, . . . to appoint a board of health to consist of not less than three nor more than seven persons for such village, and a competent physician to be the health officer thereof."

"The supervisors, overseers of the poor and justices of the peace or the major part of them of each town in the aforesaid counties, shall be a board of health for such town; and they shall forthwith appoint some competent physician to be the health officer for such town."[1]

The trustees of any village or the town authorities of places not in the counties specified were also given power to constititute themselves a board of health.

There was no intention at this time of permanently establishing any such elaborate scheme of local boards of health. The Act was to be in force only until February 1833, though circumstances required its renewal for a second year, and in 1835 a recurrence of the cholera led to its re-enactment for still another year.[2] But while the first act made the expenses incurred by the local boards a charge on the counties, the first renewing act provided that expenses for removing local nuisances should be borne by the city, village or town concerned; and the second provided that *all* expenses should be paid by the city, village or town.

This first attempt at anything like a general system of local health authorities contained no provision for any central control or direction. The system was completely decentralized. One result is that it is impossible to learn how far the

---

[1] *Laws of* 1832, c. 333.   [2] *Ibid.*, 1833, c. 221; *Ibid.*, 1835, c. 103.

provisions of the Act were obeyed. In the light of later history, it seems probable that even the mandatory clauses were to a large extent a dead letter.

A second visitation of cholera in 1849 led to the permanent adoption by the legislature of the system of local boards of health. As soon as the probability of an epidemic became known, the Governor was authorized to revive by proclamation the law of 1832;[1] but after the experience of the second epidemic a permanent statute was passed of broader scope than the Act of 1832. By this statute, local boards of health were required to be organized in every village; and in towns, the supervisor and justice of the peace were to constitute a local board of health "whenever in the opinion of a majority of said board the public good requires it."[2] As in the Act of 1832, there was no attempt at establishing any supervision or control over the local authorities.

This thoroughly decentralized and practically optional scheme remained the basis of the rural health administration for thirty years. At the end of that time perhaps twenty of the 947 townships and twice as many of the incorporated villages in the State had some form of sanitary government, and but few of these local boards exhibited any activity.[3] Probably it was never expected that any general system of local boards would be permanently established under the Act of 1850. That law was enacted in fear of a particular invasion of cholera, and when that had passed, in the public

<hr />

[1] *Laws of* 1849, c. 364.

[2] *Ibid.*, 1850, c. 324. Under this statute the expenses of these local boards were made a charge on the counties; but in 1854 (c. 169) $300 was fixed as the limit which one town might impose on the county. In 1868 (c. 761) all expenses of local boards of health were made a charge on the town, village or city. In 1867 (c. 790) the powers of the local boards of health were somewhat increased.

[3] *Reports of the State Board of Health*, ii, 13.

opinion of the time, all need for the local boards in the rural districts had disappeared.

The need for health legislation apart from the special precautions in times of epidemic was, however, beginning to be realized. In 1860[1] the vaccination of all school children was made obligatory, the enforcement of the law resting with the school trustees; in 1864 a law prohibiting the adulteration of milk was enacted;[2] and in 1869 a general law on the subject of the drainage of swamp lands took the place of the frequent special laws that had been enacted at every session of the legislature since the beginning of the century.[3]

In the cities, where, of course, the need was much greater, there were local boards of health, established under the provisions of the various city charters. In response to inquiries sent out by a committee of the American Public Health Association in 1872, reports were received from boards of health in eleven of the twenty-four New York cities.[4] All of these seemed to display some activity, but only in New York and Buffalo was there any considerable corps of assistants to the health officer. In 1880 each of the cities had a local board, but in by far the greater number of these the health officers held their places rather as a matter of favor than of fitness; hence, in only a few of the cities was there any efficient health administration.[5]

During the years 1866 to 1870 New York City, Brooklyn, Staten Island, and parts of Westchester and Queens counties were formed into a metropolitan sanitary district, with a board of health appointed by the Governor of the State.

---

[1] *Laws of* 1860, c. 438.   [2] *Ibid.,* 1864, c. 544; *ibid.,* 1878, c. 220.

[3] *Ibid.,* 1869, c. 220; *ibid.,* 1871, c. 303; *ibid.,* 1873, c. 243.

[4] In Auburn, Brooklyn, Buffalo, Cohoes, Elmira, Hudson, Newburgh, New York, Poughkeepsie, Rochester and Troy. *Proceedings of the American Public Health Association,* i, 506.

[5] *Reports of the State Board of Health,* ii, 13.

This, however, is an instance of state control over the local government of the metropolitan district rather than an illustration of any tendency to establish a central control over the local health authorities throughout the State. In any case, the state control lasted for but a few years, and with this single temporary exception the administration of health laws, other than quarantine regulations, remained entirely in the hands of independent local authorities, until the creation of the State Board of Health in 1880.

From the time of the organization of the Massachusetts State Board of Health in 1869, leading physicians and public-spirited citizens in New York had been urging the necessity of the creation of a state sanitary system, under a central board of health.[1]   Other states soon followed the example of Massachusetts, but it was not until after ten years of discussion, when twenty-two other state boards had been established, that the New York legislature passed the necessary law.

The specific powers of the New York State Board of Health as first created were limited.[2]   It was to "take cognizance of the interests of health and life among the people of the State," to make inquiries and investigations into nuisances and causes of disease, and to have supervision of the state system of registration of births, marriages and deaths.   The jurisdiction of the state board did not impair in any way the authority of the local boards, but was rather intended to supplement their powers in matters that could not be attended to by local authorities.   Even in supervising the registration of vital statistics the central authority did not at first have any compulsory powers.

Once established, however, the State Board of Health exerted an educational influence over local boards much

---

[1] E. Harris, in Chadbourne and Moore, *The Public Service of New York*, ii, 447.

[2] *Laws of* 1880, c. 322; c. 512.

wider than the authority conferred by the text of the law; and it so proved its usefulness that new powers have been conferred on it, increasing both its work of direct administration and its power of supervision, though in no case supplanting the local authorities. One of the earliest and most important tasks of the state board was to organize and stimulate into activity the local boards. In 1881[1] it received authority to direct the supervisors to call town boards of health into life; and by calling attention to the law of 1850, requiring the formation of village boards of health, it brought many of these into existence. In 1885[2] the supervisory authority of the state board was increased by requiring local boards to use the forms for registration of vital statistics prepared by it; by requiring local boards to report facts relating to infectious diseases; by authorizing the state board to summon a meeting of any local board to consider some specific subject recommended by the state board; and by empowering the state board to compel local boards to perform their duties by applying to the courts for a mandamus.

A further power was conferred at first by special acts, and in 1889 by a general act, requiring villages proposing to build sewage systems to submit their plans for approval to the State Board of Health.[3] And again, by the Revised Public Health Law of 1893, local boards are required to report certain classes of diseases in addition to vital statistics, and in case of the neglect of local authorities to establish a local board of health, the state board may perform directly the duties of a local board.

By means of this legislation the various local boards, from being independent units, have been co-ordinated and com-

[1] *Laws of* 1881, c. 431.	[2] *Ibid.*, 1885, c. 270.

[3] *Ibid.*, 1886, c. 608; *ibid.*, 1887, c. 609; *ibid.*, 1888, c. 311; *ibid.*, 1889, c. 375

bined into a state system, under a central board which stimulates them to action, is an advisory resource, and in case of last resort can exercise mandatory powers. This supervision exercised only to keep the local authorities active in the discharge of their duties is radically different from a system of centralized administration, and the powers of the central board are vastly less than those possessed by the English Local Government Board over public health regulations.

Along with this development of the supervisory authority of the state board has gone an increase in the powers of direct administration entrusted to it; and at the same time an increase in the powers of the local authorities. The statute of 1850 remains the basis of the authority vested in the local boards, but later amendments [1] have added much to their jurisdiction and their powers of enforcement. To the state board has been given the duty of enforcing new statutes, which would otherwise have been left to enforce themselves, such as the Foods & Drugs Adulteration Acts, the Act forbidding the use of explosive oils below certain tests, the investigation and suppression of tuberculosis in cows.[2] These Acts mark an increase in the sphere of central administration, but this increase has been through the extension of governmental activities, and not by limiting the powers of the local officials.

To sum up the leading points of this historical sketch. The first health regulations in New York consisted of executive orders establishing quarantine—a thoroughly centralized system. In 1755 the legislature began to enact laws on this subject, but the administration of quarantine has continued to be wholly centralized. Further health legislation was

[1] *Laws of* 1881, c. 431; *ibid.*, 1885, c. 270; *ibid.*, 1888, c. 146; *ibid.*, 1897, c. 138, 169.

[2] *Ibid.*, 1881, c. 407; *ibid.*, 1885, c. 176; *ibid.*, 1886, c. 407; *ibid.*, 1882, c. 292; *ibid.*, 1892, c. 487; *ibid.*, 1895, c. 1031.

enacted by laws for special localities and enforced by local
boards of health. In 1832 a complete system of local
boards was temporarily provided for, and in 1850 a permanent statute of the same nature was enacted; but although
these Acts were mandatory in form, there being no authority
to enforce them but few local boards were established;
while the custom of creating city boards of health and
defining their powers by special legislation continued to be
followed. In 1880 a State Board of Health was established
with very limited powers. Later legislation has increased
the powers of both local boards and the state board, and has
also added to the supervisory authority of the state board
over the local organizations. This recent development is
not in the nature of centralization, but shows rather the
evolution of a system of strong local organizations subject
to central advice and control.

2. *The State Board of Health*

The State Board of Health is composed of three classes of
members; first, three State health commissioners appointed
by the Governor; secondly, three city health officers, two
selected by the Governor, the health officer of New York
acting *ex-officio;* thirdly, the Attorney General, the State
Engineer and Surveyor, and the health officer of the port of
New York, *ex-officiis*. The last named official is appointed
by the Governor for a term of four years; the other five
members named by the Governor are appointed for three
years; the two State officials are elected for two-year terms;
and the New York City health officer is appointed by the
city health board for six years. In practice, the State commissioners have been frequently re-appointed, one member
having served for nine years, and the average term of service before 1895 being five years. None of the members of
the board receives a salary as such.

The board forms its own internal organization. One of the State health commissioners is elected President, and a Secretary is appointed, at a salary of $4500, who directs the routine administrative work. Quarterly meetings of the board are provided for, but in practice from ten to twelve meetings are held each year. Seven standing committees, on each of which the President and Secretary are members, are appointed for different phases of the board's activities.

Considering first those functions of the board by which it exercises a supervision and control over local authorities, it may be noted again that in the early years of the board its powers of this nature were only advisory, and that it possessed little real authority. This limitation of its powers probably arose from the distrust of any marked centralization in a field of administration formerly left wholly to local action; and this distrust made it important for the board to make clear the difference between its authority and a centralized administration. Accordingly we find from the first an emphasis on this distinction, a declaration of a purpose to proceed by means of consultation and advice rather than by command. In the first report, the statement is made that "without any abridgment of the rights and privileges of local government of the towns, villages and cities of the Commonwealth, the State Board of Health has been organized and put in operation,"[1] Two years later the same point was emphasized in these words:[2] "Though not wanting in certain kinds of authority, the policy of this department of the State's service has mostly been directly the converse of centralization or dictation. From first to last, and from centre to circumference, the service has been, and will continue to be, chiefly a work of studious instruction and guidance in the work required."

[1] *Reports of the State Board of Health*, i, 94.   [2] *Ibid.*, iii, 63.

The work accomplished by the board by this method of advice and instruction has been by no means insignificant. One of the first tasks undertaken was the preparation and distribution among the various local authorities of a compend of the public health laws in force. By thus calling attention to the provisions of the almost forgotten statutes, the organization and activity of local boards of health in hundreds of towns and villages were secured.[1]   In addition, by preparing, distributing and recommending sets of local sanitary ordinances, the state board made clear to the new, and also to older local boards, that there were opportunities for their activity even with no epidemic disease in sight. Then, too, on account of the frequent changes in the personnel of the local boards, bringing persons unfamiliar with the duties of sanitary administration into office, there soon developed a constant inquiry and correspondence with the central office regarding the routine of work, and the most elementary questions of sanitary requirements.[2]   This work of sanitary correspondence with the local boards, by giving them the accumulated experience of the state board, greatly added to the usefulness of the former.

The inquiries from the local authorities were not long confined to matters which could be answered off-hand.   The advice and assistance of the state board is frequently asked on questions of sanitary improvements requiring more technical knowledge than the localities can command.[3]   In such cases, the policy of the state board has been to make, through its sanitary inspectors, engineers and chemists, the

[1] Town Boards of Health consist of the Supervisor, Town Clerk and four Justices of the Peace, *ex-officiis*, and one citizen member. In the incorporated villages and cities there are generally no *ex-officio* members, and the number in the board varies. Each board chooses a health officer, (who must be a physician) and a registrar of vital statistics.

[2] *Reports of the State Board of Health*, vi, 6.   [3] *Ibid.*, v, 20.

necessary expert examination, to decide as to the necessity for the proposed works, and as to their general character, leaving to the community to make its own plans in detail.

Not only have the local boards thus asked for advice and technical assistance from the state board, they have also appealed to it to secure redress from unsanitary conditions beyond their control.[1] In some cases the complaint is against conditions beyond their jurisdiction; in others the cause of the trouble may be a powerful railway corporation which pays little heed to the remonstrances of the local board of health in a small town. Here again, the state board makes a direct investigation, and its recommendations for sanitary improvements have been generally followed. Complaints from individuals as to the inaction of their local authorities in the face of necessary sanitary reform are similarly investigated, and such improvements as are required recommended to the localities. In many such cases there has been a local conflict of opinion, and the decision of the state board as a competent and impartial authority is accepted without demur. In some matters, too, the board can compel the acceptance of its recommendations, but this power belongs to another phase of the subject. Even where it has had no mandatory authority, the State Board of Health has accomplished much through its educational and advisory influence.

The only provision in the legislation of 1880 requiring the local boards to come into relations to the state board, was in regard to the registration of vital statistics. The collection of these statistics was to be under the direction of local boards of health, and the state board was to prepare the necessary forms for preserving the data collected. The state board prepared the forms and distributed them over the

state; but the actual returns received were at first so meagre
that not until April, 1884, was it found practicable to attempt
any compilation of the returns, which even then were very
far short of completeness.[1] The amendments to the law in
1885 required the local boards to secure and report the
record of vital statistics in accordance with the methods and
forms prescribed by the state board. Under this provision
the returns improved in completeness; but in 1889 there
were still 80 towns which made no reports, and for the por
tion of the State outside of the cities the low death rate of
13.10 per 1000, showed that the returns were still deficient.[2]
The number of towns making no returns has now diminished
to fifteen or twenty, but the superintendent of this department of the state board's work reports in 1896[3] that "undoubtedly many local boards have not reported fully" on
the mortality in their district. On the whole, however, the
death statistics have been reasonably complete for the last
eight years; but the data on births and marriages have not
yet warranted their compilation and publication.

The later legislation has required the local boards to report promptly to the state board, in addition to vital statistics, facts relating to infectious and epidemic diseases, and
by the law of 1893 all cases of infectious and contagious
diseases must be reported monthly, and the number of cases
of consumption must be reported annually.

The statistics secured in this way are not only valuable for
purposes of comparison, but an increased death-rate in any
locality will also draw the attention of the state board to the
need of investigating local sanitary conditions, and exercising its functions of positive control over the localities.

In addition to the regular reports of vital statistics, city and
village authorities desiring to construct or extend sewerage

[1] *Reports of the State Board of Health*, v, 2.
[2] *Ibid.*, ix, 35, 51.   [3] *Ibid.*, xvi, 448.

systems must have their plans approved by the State Board
of Health. With this approval of their plans, the villages
are now authorized by general law to proceed with the construction, where formerly a special statute was necessary for
each village system and even for each extension of an existing system. The increase of administrative supervision has,
therefore, been accompanied by the diminution of legislative
control, and has to the same extent relieved the legislature
of a considerable amount of special legislation.

On the submission of plans and specifications for any proposed sewerage system or extension, these are referred to one
of the consulting engineers of the board, and on his examination and report the board takes action on the question of
approval. In the first six years under the general law, 71
cities and villages submitted to the State Board of Health
plans and specifications for proposed sewerage systems or extensions of existing systems. The one statute has supplied
all the legislation necessary, where under the old method 71
different Acts would have been passed; and there can be
no question that the method of expert examination by the
consulting engineers of the state board ensures more scientific and efficient sewer constructions than any investigations
made by a temporary legislative committee. Moreover,
the new method makes it much easier for sewer systems to
be built, whether the initiative comes from the localities
voluntarily, or after suggestion from the state board. The
wisdom of the law is well exemplified by the number of
plans that have been brought to the state board for review.

The degree of positive or compulsory authority which the
State Board of Health can now exert over local boards is
limited to certain specific provisions of the law. By means
of these it can (1) require local boards to take action in any
particular case recommended by the State Board; (2) over-
rule acts of local boards where they affect the public health

beyond the jurisdiction of the local board; (3) secure the enforcement of any duty prescribed by statute on local boards, through the use of mandamus proceedings in the courts; and (4) assume direct control where no local board is organized.

Under these provisions a considerable degree of positive central control over the local boards might be exerted except for two causes. The legislative appropriation for the expenses of the state board sets a limit to its activity in this as in other directions; but equally potent is the fact that the policy of the board has been to use its mandatory and compulsory powers as little as possible. It has acted on the principle of "working through the local organizations established by law, preserving their autonomy and independence, settling their disputes, supplementing their deficiencies and endeavoring to elevate the plane of their usefulness."[1] Thus, the whole tendency has been to leave the actual sanitary administration in the hands of the local authorities, and to make the central board an educational bureau, rather than an office for issuing mandatory orders to the local boards.[2] The absence of any strong centralizing tendency may be explained in part by the board form of organization, and by the presence of local health officers on the central board; but the unanimity of opinion on the subject is a strong indication that the energetic exercise of the compulsory powers would be unwise.

The scope of the direct administrative authority possessed by the State Board of Health has already been seen in noting the grants of powers made by the legislature;[3] and it is only necessary here to call attention to the various means used to carry out these powers. The compilation, indexing and publication of the vital statistics collected from the local authori-

[1] *Reports of the State Board of Health*, viii, 9.

[2] *Ibid.*, i, 101; iii, 63; x, 36.   [3] See p. 132.

ties requires several clerks and assistants at the central office of the board. A small force of chemists is employed for making analyses of foods and drugs to discover adulterations. There are also several consulting engineers (of the State Engineer's staff) employed in making investigations on drainage, pollution of water supplies and general sanitary conditions. More important investigations, including those on epidemics of contagious diseases, are made by the medical expert of the board or by the secretary.

In these various investigations no sharp distinction is made between cases involving the relations of the state board to local boards, and those of larger interests involving state action to suppress unsanitary conditions. One noted instance of sanitary improvement far beyond the control of any local authority is the suppression of the Newton Creek and Hunter's Point (Long Island) nuisances by order of the Governor, after investigation by the state board. Three counties, three cities and fifty millions of capital invested in the offending industries presented such varied and conflicting interests that only through the action of a state authority could the necessary sanitary regulations be prescribed and enforced.[1] The drainage of extensive areas of overflowed and miasmatic lands presents another problem as yet largely unsettled, but which is far beyond the scope of any local authority to remedy. A special investigation into the existence and cause of tuberculosis in cattle, undertaken by the State Board of Health, led to the appointment in 1894 of a commission to carry on the investigation. In 1895[2] the state board was authorized to appoint three special cattle inspectors to continue a systematic investigation of all dairy cattle with a view of killing tuberculous animals.

The appointment of special inspectors by the State Board

---

[1] *Reports of the State Board of Health*, iv, 23.   [2] *Laws of* 1895, c. 1013.

of Health in the summers of 1892 and 1893,[1] when an invasion of cholera was apprehended, indicates that in time of epidemic, when the whole state is seriously threatened by an outbreak in any locality, the general and vaguely defined powers of the board over the health of the state will bring about a great increase in the sphere of direct administration. In ordinary times it concerns itself only with special cases which threaten the health of more than one community.

The State Board of Health has also the power of issuing certain administrative regulations in connection with the enforcement of various statutes. It makes rules and regulations for the protection of water supplies from contamination, to guard against the dangerous use of explosive oils, and allowing certain technical adulterations in food and drugs which it considers harmless and not inadvisable. These regulations, not for subordinates nor for local officials, but for the general public, correspond to the administrative ordinances of European countries, and indicate that the New York legislature has come to recognize some sphere of detailed regulation which can be determined better by an administrative than by a legislative authority.

3. *The Results of Central Supervision*

The most evident results of the work of the State Board of Health are to be seen in the organization of the local health authorities throughout the State. In 1880 there were less than fifty local boards of health in the entire State, and these, except in half a dozen of the largest cities, were inactive and inefficient. Within two years the secretary of the board stated that a thousand local boards had been organized,[2] thus claiming that by 1882 practically every town in

---

[1] *Reports of the State Board of Health*, xiii, 15.

[2] Dr. E. Harris in Chadbourne and Moore, *The Public Service of the State of New York*, ii, 452.

the State had its local board.   The great deficiency in registration returns indicates pretty clearly that active local
boards were by no means at work then, nor for several years
afterwards.   But in 1892 the state board published a list of
the members of the town and village local boards, showing
that the organization throughout the State was by that time
complete, and the registration statistics prove that they are
active to the point of securing returns of mortality.   Moreover there is evidence to show that these local boards are
active in other directions in looking after the sanitary conditions of their communities.   From reports received in 1892
the state board considered that it was " clearly evident that
the local boards have greatly improved in all that goes to
make effective and trustworthy guardians of public health.
The various communities have awakened to a realization of
the importance of these boards, and, as a rule, members are
selected from the best class of citizens, men of personal
integrity with the welfare of their communities at heart.
These boards, in turn, select as health officers physicians of
good standing, and the wisdom of these selections has been
made manifest by the excellent work of the past year."[1]

A more effective test of the efficiency of the local boards
of health, and at the same time of the results of the creation
of the state board, will, however, be be found by considering
the evidences of improvement in the sanitary condition of
the State.   The condition in 1880, if by no means so
alarming as the situation in England in 1848, was far from
satisfactory.   Among the features of the sanitary situation
were an " increasing prevalence of miasmatic diseases . . .
the frequent recurrence of small-pox and diphtheria in
widely separated communities, the appearance of scarlet
fever in every county of the State, and the frequent preva-

_____
[1] *Reports of the State Board of Health*, xiii, 11.

lence of measles and whooping cough." [1] It has been estimated that in two decades before 1880 there had been
70,000 deaths from diphtheria alone. The condition of
affairs in the village of Johnstown during a diphtheria epidemic in 1878 shows the dangers of the existing situation
and the need for some central health authority to induce
such localities to take the necessary preventive measures.

"No public measures against the disease were instituted,
except that the schools were closed for a period of three
weeks at the height of the epidemic. The funerals were
public, corpse-watching was a custom, and children were
pall-bearers at the funerals. Visiting among the sick does
not seem to have been feared, and was freely indulged.
The disease once introduced spread rapidly; after a time
the school-houses seem to have become foci of infection.
. . . One family had diphtheria three times during the
three years, and six families twice." [2] Under these conditions it is not surprising to learn that in a population of
5,200 there were 219 cases and 61 deaths.

In another instance nearly one-third of all the inhabitants
of a large incorporated village were found suffering from
malarial fever, arising from stagnant pools and sodden
grounds a little distance beyond the corporate limits of the
village. It was considered that fully a half of the entire
population of the State was living in the immediate presence
of such sources of malaria as could be removed by the adoption of drainage measures and sanitary improvements. [3]

The extent of the improvement in sanitary conditions and
of greater efficiency in sanitary administration since the days
when such conditions were possible, can be best tested by
noticing the extent to which diseases caused by unsanitary
conditions have decreased. The usual test for sanitary conditions is the zymotic death rate, and this rate by giving

[1] *Reports of the State Board of Health*, ii, 3.   [2] *Ibid.*, i, 118.   [3] *Ibid.*, ii, 16, 28.

approximate indications possesses considerable value. But
some diseases classed as zymotic, such as whooping-cough
and measles, are much less amenable to sanitary measures
than others, as diphtheria and fevers.[1]   More accurate tests
can therefore be obtained by considering, in addition to the
total zymotic death rate, the death rate for the particular
diseases which are most subject to control by sanitary regulations.   In the following table these death rates in New
York are presented for each year since the reports to the
State Board of Health have been published.   By comparing
the number of deaths from the specified causes with the
total number of deaths reported, the error from deficiencies
in the reports may be considered to have been avoided,
since we may fairly assume that the unreported deaths contain about the same proportion of zymotic deaths as the
cases reported.

Mortality Statistics, New York State.[2]

	Deaths reported from all causes.	Rate per 1000 population of deaths reported.	Number of deaths in every 1000 deaths from								
			Zymotic Diseases.	Consumption.	Diarrhœal Diseases.	Diphtheria.	Typhoid Fever.	Malaria.	Scarlet Fever.	Whooping Cough.	Measles.
1885..	80,407	......	222.17	139.76	90.80	56.06	13.27				
1886..	86,801	......	217.23	137.66	80.97	64.48	13.47				
1887..	96,453	......	227.80	120.35	96.00	67.24	13.75				
1888..	104,119	17.62	220.80	118.55	84.00	61.73	14.18	8.2	23.0	8.8	8.2
1889..	103,969	17.00	210.34	120.01	79.56	56.12	14.86	7.1	22.2	12.8	9.5
1890..	118,552	18.85	164.80	118.37	72.48	42.07	13.79	6.2	7.0	9.9	9.9
1891..	122,398	19.20	178.80	109.50	74.15	40.78	15.52	5.2	17.8	6.8	10.1
1892..	128,015	19.70	181.18	104.80	72.72	46.86	13.25	4.9	17.4	6.9	10.5
1893..	122,841	19.00	181.85	107.21	73.30	48.00	13.51	4.2	14.1	9.9	6.5
1894..	119,774	18.25	193.00	106.85	75.77	55.77	13.87	3.5	11.1	8.8	7.9
1895..	121,297	18.60	159.60	109.65	74.55	41.00	14.10	2.6	7.1	9.5	9.3
1896..	120,683	18.50	156.00	110.54	72.70	38.00	12.75	3.7	6.3	8.3	12.4
1897..	117,075	18.40	140.00	108.13	62.50	35.15	11.55	3.2	7.2	7.1	7.5

[1] Newsholme, *Vital Statistics*, p. 174.

[2] Compiled from reports of the State Board of Health.

From these figures it appears that the total zymotic death rate, though subject to some variations, has on the whole rapidly declined during the past twelve years. In the columns for particular diseases, the variations in the statistics for measles and whooping cough illustrate what has been said as to the difficulty of controlling these diseases by sanitary measures. On the other hand, the proportion of deaths from malarial diseases, from scarlet fever, and from diphtheria —those most subject to sanitary control—show a large and steady decrease, the proportion of deaths from these three causes being only a half of that twelve years ago. The deaths from diarrhœal diseases and typhoid fever also show a noticeable decrease. In these respects, then, the results show that the enforcement of sanitary regulations and the suppression of unhealthful conditions are more efficiently carried out at present than formerly. And the cause of that greater efficiency of the local authorities is largely, if not mainly, due to the activities of the State Board of Health in stimulating the local authorities by its educational propaganda and occasionally by the use of its more mandatory powers. In the case of the diminution in the proportion of deaths from diphtheria the state board makes the specific claim, that it " is pretty certainly due to the more intelligent management of these epidemics, and the enforcement of quarantine under the direction of this board."[1]

But while we recognize this improvement in sanitary conditions, the study of the situation shows that further improvement might have been made. The proportion of deaths from typhoid fever and from diarrhœal diseases has not been reduced to any very great extent, and the present ratio is much higher than exists elsewhere. Nor is the situation in respect to scarlet fever and diphtheria wholly satisfactory. In

---

[1] *Reports of the State Board of Health*, xiii, 13.

1895, the former was prevalent in three-quarters of the counties of the State; only three counties were entirely free of the latter, and in twenty-five of the sixty counties it was prevalent to a considerable degree.

These facts show that much yet remains to be done in the way of sanitary improvement, and that local boards are deficient either in authority or in energetic activity. If the former, we should expect to find appeals to the legislature for an increase in their statutory powers, and in the absence of that we may conclude that much could be gained by further increasing their activity. As in all questions in this country, much can be done by arousing public opinion; but another method is also at hand—to increase the powers of the State Board of Health. Nor is it necessary in order to gain the desired ends that this increase should be along the lines of direct centralization of health administration, nor even of an increase in the mandatory powers of the state board. Under American conditions the general policy of the state board to act as an advisory rather than a mandatory bureau seems likely to accomplish the most valuable sanitary results, and much can be accomplished by extending the activities of the state board along the lines of its policy in the past.

More specifically, the establishment of a systematic visitation of the localities by officers of the central bureau would keep the local boards at a much higher grade of activity and efficiency. During the summers of 1892 and 1893, when there was the possibility of cholera invading the State from Europe, such inspectors were appointed by the state board for the districts along the Canadian border, where the possibility of the disease making an entrance was greatest. The work of these inspectors, the board announced, "has resulted in other good than merely preparing for an epidemic. It has aroused more interest in preventive medicine, and added

to the efficiency of local boards by stimulating them to more
decisive action in sanitation. The advantage of having authorized representatives of the state board to visit and consult with local officers encourages the latter in their duties,
is a practical assurance of State aid, and gives to the local
authorities an assistance which counteracts local pressure." [1]
In the report of the State Board of Health for 1895 Dr.
Curtis, in his review of "The Sanitary Condition of the
State," urges that "The state board could effect a greater
fidelity to their duties by keeping in closer touch with the
local boards through the personal and frequent visitation of
an inspector from this board." [2] We may add that with such
a force of inspectors the state board might find it possible to
apply the mandatory powers already possessed to a much
larger number of cases; but it is not necessary to emphasize
this feature. The most important results would be those
accomplished through the educational and advisory influence as described in the extract quoted.

Although the state board has recognized the use to which
such a force of state inspectors would be put, it has not
urged on the legislature the importance of making this extension of their work. The main difficulty would be to
secure the necessary appropriation from the legislature, and
undoubtedly the suspicion of centralization would be added
to the spirit of economy as an opposing force. Certainly,
however, so long as the state board itself does not insist on
this further step, it is not likely to come voluntarily from the
legislature. If the State Board of Health will advocate what
it has already recognized as a natural and rational development of its functions, it is possible that the opposition in the
legislature might not prove so vigorous as has been antici-
pated.

[1] *Reports of the State Board of Health*, xiv, 9.   [2] *Ibid.*, xvi, 448.

CHAPTER V

TAXATION AND LOCAL FINANCE

1. *The Evolution of Decentralized Tax Administration*

THE earliest form of tax administration in New Netherlands was the simple and centralized method of collection by
the financial agent of the Dutch West India Company. The
duties on imports and exports established at the time the
company gave up its monopoly of trade in 1640,[1] and the
excises instituted in 1644 and 1647,[2] were collected by this
officer, known as the Schout Fiscal, who beside his duties as
tax collector was also sheriff and prosecuting attorney for
the colony. He was appointed either by the authorities in
Holland or by the Director General.

About the middle of the decade 1650–1660, the method
of collecting these customs and excise taxes was changed to
that of farming them out to the highest bidder. This was
done with the excise as early as 1653; and in 1655 the
amount of the excise farm for New Amsterdam was 5030
guilders, for Beverwyck, 2013 guilders.[3] The customs
seemed to have been first farmed in 1656 for 3000 florins.
The directors in Holland did not approve of this last change;[4]
but Stuyvesant continued his own policy, and the farming of
customs as well as excise duties continued until the English

---

[1] Freedoms and Exemptions of 1640, in *New York Colonial Documents*, i, 121.
Laws and Ordinances of New Netherlands, p. 31.

[2] *Laws and Ordinances of New Netherlands*, 1644, p. 38; 1647, p. 67.

[3] Brodhead, *History of New York*, i, 610.

[4] *New York Colonial Documents*, xiv, 389.

occupation.[1]   During the last ten years of the Dutch government the tithes for the support of the ministers and school-
masters were collected by the province government. The
magistrates of the different villages, mainly on Long Island,
compounded with the Director and Council for a lump sum
in produce,[2] while the assessment and levy of this total on
individuals was under the control of the local authorities.

When the English gained possession of the Dutch colony
in 1664, the existing system of taxation was retained, and in
the collection of the excise the method of farming the tax
was also continued.[3]   But for the administration of the im-
port and export duties a Collector and Receiver General
was appointed, who acted also as the general financial agent
of the Duke of York.   This officer occupied a position very
largely independent of the Governor; he was appointed by
the authorities in England, and although the Governors on
several occasions exercised a power of suspension, this was
only on charges of flagrant misconduct.[4]   The financial administration was not subject to the active control and direction of the Governor, so that thus early we find the beginning of independent and unrelated administrative bureaus,—
a characteristic feature of State government to-day.

Besides the customs and excise taxes, Governor Nicolls
ordered the levy of a general property tax of one penny in
the pound, to meet the expenses of the new county courts
he had established.   This tax was not a province tax, but a
" publique rate " for county expenses, and the receipts did

---

[1] *Laws and Ordinances of New Netherlands*, 1663, p. 441.

[2] *New York Colonial Documents*, xiv, 421, 503, 531.

[3] The Acts of the Assembly after 1691 speak of paying the excise duties at the
office of excise, but other references show that the farming system was continued,
so that this office of excise must have been the office of the farmer. Cf. *New York
Colonial Documents*, iii, 335; *Colonial Laws*, 1699, c. 68.

[4] *New York Colonial Documents*, iii, 221, 335, 422; iv, 320, 1143.

not go to the Receiver General. As, however, it was from this county rate that the general property tax for province purposes was later developed, its early history is of interest to our subject. The local machinery of assessment and collection already employed in the English settlements on Long Island for poor rates and local expenses was naturally adopted for this county tax. On February 26th, 1665, Nicolls issued a warrant to the High Sheriff of Yorkshire, directing him to send warrants to the high constables of the ridings into which it had been divided, requiring them to send warrants to the constables and overseers in each town to levy and collect the tax.¹ The Duke of York's Laws promulgated later in the year, regulated the system of tax administration in more detail. The assessment and collection of the tax continued to be vested in the overseers chosen by each town; but they were subject to the supervision and control of officers appointed by the Governor. The assessment had to be at certain fixed rates for each kind of property, and the assessment lists were to be examined and approved by the High Sheriff, and by him transmitted to the Governor.² The constables were required to make returns to the High Sheriff, and the accounts of both sheriff and constables must be audited at the semi-annual courts of sessions of the justices of the peace.³

The Dongan Assembly of 1683 repealed the existing laws regulating the county rates, and provided for an elected authority in each city, town and county for " supervising the publique affairs and charge of each respective City, Towne and County."⁴ Probably, with the suspension of assemblies,

¹ *New York Colonial Documents*, xiv, 573.

² *Duke of Yorke's Laws*, in J. B. Linn, *Charter and Laws of the Province of Pennsylvania*, pp. 44, 48, 49.

³ *Ibid.*, Amendments of 1673, p. 73.

⁴ *Colonial Laws of New York*, 1683, c. 6; c. 9.

these vague provisions were neglected, and the former methods continued to be used for the county rate. The legislature of 1691, however, abolished the control over the local
officers exercised by the appointed sheriffs and justices of
the peace. Instead, there was to be "a certain freeholder
. . . chosen in each respective Town . . . to supervise and
examine the public and necessary charge."[1] In 1701 this
law was repealed, and the justices of the peace were again
directed to supervise the county tax;[2] but it is doubtful if
this was enforced. Town records show that supervisors
continued to be elected,[3] and the famous Supervisor Law of
1703 assumes the law of 1691 to be still in force.[4] At any
rate, after 1703 the elected supervisors were the final authority in the administration of the county rate. They were to
determine the proportion of the county tax to be collected
in each town; and the town assessors and collectors were
required to make the rate and collect the tax according to
these apportionments. The money collected was to be paid
to the county treasurer, who was appointed and his accounts
audited yearly by the supervisors. The only control over
the supervisors was in the courts, which could impose a
penalty for neglect or refusal to perform their duties, on
complaint of any person injured. If, however, any town
neglected to choose any of the officers provided for, the justices of the peace in the county were authorized to appoint
persons to act. These last provisions would become effective only in exceptional cases, and the ordinary administration of the county tax was now completely decentralized.

The first general property tax imposed on the entire
province was a tax of one penny in the pound ordered by

[1] *Colonial Laws of New York*, 1691, c. 6.   [2] *Ibid.*, 1701, c. 96.

[3] *Records of Easthampton*, iii, pp. 28, 61.

[4] *Colonial Laws of New York*, 1703, c. 133.

the Dongan Assembly of 1683, as a "free and voluntary present to the governor." The machinery of local assessment and collection which had been in use for the county rate for twenty years in Long Island, and for ten years in the rest of the province, was to be employed for this general tax; but there were also provided commissioners for each county—named in the act—who were to direct the local officials, and to equalize assessments on complaint.[1] The proceeds of the tax were to be paid over to the receiver general.

The cessation of assemblies in New York after 1684 prevented the development at this time of any regular system of provincial direct taxation; and for the next seven years the revenue was derived as before from the customs and excise duties. But when, after the English Revolution of 1689, New York became involved in a struggle with the Indians, as a part of the conflict between William III and Louis XVI, the expenses of the military campaigns necessitated new sources of revenue, and at the same time the grant of a legislative assembly to New York provided the means for raising this revenue by means of direct taxation. The extra-legal Leisler Assembly in 1690 passed two acts levying a general province tax on real and personal property;[2] the assembly called by Governor Sloughter in 1691 levied £3500, by a similar direct tax, for maintaining the troops at Albany; and for each of the following six years provincial direct taxes were levied. The taxes were, however, only for military purposes, and with the conclusion of peace ceased to be levied. The renewal of the war brought the re-appearance of the tax; and the story of the eighteenth century struggle between France and England can be traced in the

---

[1] *Colonial Laws of New York*, 1683, c. 14.   [2] *Ibid.*, i, 218.

[3] *Ibid.*, chaps. 8, 15, 20, 22, 29, 30, 39, 41, 43, 50, 51, 53, 56, 58, 63.

tax legislation of New York. During the first forty years of the century the provincial direct tax was only occasional, but in the last two periods of active struggle (1744–47, 1754–63) the levies were made annually and for much larger amounts than before.[1]

The administrative machinery provided for the collection of the tax of 1690 is unknown, as no copies of the laws have been preserved. In the law of 1691, the method followed in 1683 of utilizing the local officers for assessment and collection was again pursued; and, as in the law of 1683, there was provided a supervision over the local officials. Instead, however, of commissioners named by the legislature, this supervision was entrusted to the justices of the peace in each county, while in New York and Albany, the mayor, recorder and aldermen performed this duty. The functions of these supervising authorities consisted in apportioning the county quota—which was specified in the act—among the various towns and manors, and in ordering the local assessors to assess and levy the tax, under penalty of imprisonment. They had, however, no authority to revise or alter the individual assessments of the local assessors. The proceeds of the tax were to be paid over to the Receiver General of the Customs, but that officer had no control or supervision over the local authorities.[2] The Act of 1691 was passed on the same day as the act establishing the supervisor system; and it is significant of the different conception of the new tax, that while the supervision of the appointed justices of the peace was at this time abolished for the county tax, it should be retained for the provincial tax.

The provisions of the Act of 1691 were repeated in subsequent acts, and the underlying principle of local assessment

[1] *Colonial Laws of New York*, chaps. 112, 116, 191, 222, 447, 541, 775, 825, 832, 854, 920, 977, 988, 1082, 1472.

[2] *Ibid.*, 1691, c. 8.

and collection has been continued until to-day. The first important change was the appointment by the Assembly in 1705 of its own treasurer to receive the tax. This step strengthened the legislative control of provincial finances at the expense of the central administration, and was therefore to some extent a decentralizing measure.[1]   A more important step, however, was the abandonment of the supervision of the justices of the peace, which was definitively accomplished about the middle of the century.   In 1728, when a tax of £200 was ordered, the duty of apportioning the quota of each county among the towns, and of directing the collection of the tax, was placed, for the first time, upon the elected supervisors.[2]   No province tax had been ordered for the three years preceding this, and perhaps the smallness of the amount called for at this time made it seem useless to call on the justices to act, when the supervisors were annually performing a similar duty for the county tax. The same reason will explain the adoption of the same measures for the tax of £730, ordered in the following year.[3]   Then follows fifteen years during which no property tax was levied by the Assembly.   Beginning in 1744, large amounts were again called for; and we find that the precedents of 1728 and 1729 instead of the earlier acts were followed,[4] and complete decentralization in the administration of the provincial direct tax may be said to have been established.

The Provincial Treasurer chosen by the Assembly from 1705 on did not entirely supplant the Receiver General. At first only the direct tax was given to the first named officer, and the latter continued to receive the proceeds of

---

[1] *New York Colonial Documents*, iv, 1145; *Colonial Laws of New York*, 1706, c. 159.

[2] *Colonial Laws of New York*, 1728, c. 530.   [3] *Ibid.*, 1729, c. 541.

[4] *Ibid.*, 1744, c. 775; 1746, c. 825; c. 832; 1747, c. 854; 1755, c. 970; 1759, c. 1018.

the customs and excise duties. In 1714, however, an officer
was appointed to collect the customs and to pay them over
to the Treasurer;[1] and in the same year it was directed that
the revenue from the farm of the excise should be paid to
the Treasurer.[2] Over the local administration of the excise
the legislature also established its authority. An Act of
1709 had provided that the justices of the peace, and in the
municipal corporations the mayor, recorder and aldermen
should conduct the auction of the excise farm ;[3] but the statute
of 1714[2] named commissioners for each county who were
to let the excise farm, and to receive the payments for
transmission to the Treasurer. These changes transferred
authority from the representatives of the Crown to the representatives of the localities, and thus weakened the central
administration. To this extent the changes were in the
direction of decentralization; but it should also be noted
that as yet there was no movement toward transferring the
local administration of these taxes to officials elected in the
localities.

For a quarter of a century the system of excise administration established in 1714 was continued unchanged.
Then the legislature undertook a more direct management
of the system. The excise act of 1737[4] named the farmers
of the excise in five counties, and the amount which they
agreed to pay. In the act for 1739[5] the farmers of the excise are named for all the counties, and the system of commissioners to let the excise farm has completely disappeared.
Fifteen years later a further step in direct legislative management was taken. The preamble to this act of 1753[6] set
forth that "the present method of collecting the duty on excise by letting the same to farm is found grievous to the several retailers, by the exorbitant and excessive exactions of

[1] *Colonial Laws of New York*, c. 273.   [2] *Ibid.*, c. 284.   [3] *Ibid.*, c. 189.
[4] *Ibid.*, c. 645.   [5] *Ibid.*, c. 684.   [6] *Ibid.*, c. 944.

many of the farmers of the said duty." Accordingly, the system of farming the excise was abolished. Instead, the legislature chose two commissioners for each county, who were named in the statute and were to fix the number and appoint the retailers of liquor in their respective counties, fix the amount to be paid by each retailer and collect the revenue. The act, however, names the total amount to be paid by all the retailers in each county, thus limiting the functions of the commissioners in that respect to apportioning the amount named in the act among the various dealers. The cities of New York and Albany were made exceptions to this act by providing that there the mayor, recorder and aldermen should act as the local excise commissioners. After a single year commissioners were named for New York,[1] and in 1764 for Albany also,[2] thus closing the last links in the chain of legislative centralization in excise administration.

Thus far the revenue from the excise taxes went into the general provincial treasury,[3] and in consequence there was little tendency to transfer the local administration to officials chosen in the towns and counties. But, in 1773, the tax was suddenly changed from a province to a local tax. The excise law of that year provided that the excise revenue should go to county treasurers, highway commissioners, overseers of the poor and the city corporations, to be used for local purposes.[4] However, no change in administrative methods was made, and the excise continued for several years to be collected by the commissioners named by the legislature. It was not until 1779 that the excise administration was decentralized in accordance with the now local

---

[1] *Colonial Laws of New York*, c. 959.   [2] *Ibid.*, c. 1245.

[3] In New York City, however, there was a tavern keeper's license, which went into the city treasury. Valentine's *Manual* for 1859, pp. 504, 507.

[4] *Colonial Laws of New York*, c. 1548.

character of the tax. Under the law of that year,[1] passed
by the first State legislature, the supervisors in each county
were to act as commissioners of excise, and the revenue was
to go to the county treasurers for county expenses. In the
cities the mayor, recorder and aldermen were to act as
excise commissioners, and as the mayors were appointed by
the central government, there was still some control over the
excise system in these localities until in 1821 the choice of
mayors by the State authorities was abolished. This central
control was made even more effective in New York city by
a law of 1788[2] providing for an excise commissioner for that
city to be appointed by the Governor; and it was not until
1824 that excise administration in the metropolis was turned
over entirely to the local authorities.[3]

During the Revolutionary struggle, the customs duties
were collected by the British officers who held possession of
New York City. On the departure of the British troops a
customs act was passed,[4] establishing the same centralized
administrative system as in the colonial period. The collectors, gaugers, weighmasters and other custom-house officials were made appointees of the Governor and Council.
But this department of the State administration was soon to
disappear, for with the organization of the new federal government in 1789 the control over customs passed into its
hands, and the State customs officials ceased to act.

The joint effect of the Excise Act of 1773 and the establishment of the federal government in 1789 was to deprive

---

[1] *Laws of* 1779, c. 17.   [2] *Ibid.*, 1788, c. 48.

[3] *Ibid.*, 1824, c. 215. Excise Commissioner Lyman in his report for 1896
speaks of the Liquor Tax Law of that year as making a radical departure from the
principle of local control in use for over three hundred years. It has been shown
above that local control was not established in the counties until 1779, in the cities
the local authorities were subject to central control until 1821, and in New York
city the excise officers were state appointees until 1824.

[4] *Ibid.*, 1784, c. 10.

the State Treasury of both the Excise and the Customs duties, and left the general property tax as the only form of taxation for the State. In fact, however, the receipts from the sale of lands and quit rents were generally sufficient to meet the expenses of the State government, and after 1780 the property tax was levied only at irregular intervals. When it was used, the administrative methods of the laws since 1740 were adopted. "The amount of a tax upon the State being declared, the legislature determines the quotas to be paid by the counties, the supervisors of the counties determine the quotas of the towns, which last are apportioned to individuals by assessors."[1]

A brief experiment in centralization is seen in the Act of 1799,[2] regulating in more detail the method of assessing and collecting the general property tax. By this law three commissioners of taxes were to be appointed for each county, to supervise the assessment; and, instead of the rough equalization by determining county and town quotas, these commissioners were given authority to equalize the assessments of the town officers. After only two years this system was abandoned. The supervision of the assessment was again placed in the hands of the boards of supervisors, but the equalizing authority of the commissioners was not given them, and even their former power of determining town quotas no longer appears.[3] In these respects the town officers were given a larger independence in making their local assessments. A provision in the law of 1789 requiring copies of the assessment rolls to be sent to the State Comptroller was, however, retained; and this gave that official an opportunity to compare the returns made by the collectors with actual assessments made. In 1804, this central supervision was made slightly stronger by requiring the town as-

---

[1] Wolcott's *Report on State Finances*, in *American State Papers, Finance*, i, 425.

[2] *Laws of* 1799, c. 72.   [3] *Ibid.*, 1801, c. 179.

sessors to use blank forms of assessment rolls to be provided by the Comptroller.[1] Provisions were also made in these laws to compel delinquent collectors to obey the law, but the method of enforcement was always by judicial action before the courts, and the State administrative officers could act only to the extent of bringing suit.

We have now traced the development of tax administration in New York to the definitive establishment of the decentralized system. Beginning with a series of customs and excise taxes collected by the mediæval farming method, this gave way during the colonial period first to a direct centralized administration of customs, and later to a legislative centralization of both customs and excises. In addition to these earlier taxes there developed a system of county taxation administered by local authorities; and when the provincial assemblies found it necessary to resort to direct taxes, the local machinery for collecting these local taxes was used. By the middle of the eighteenth century the slight supervision of the appointed justices of the peace was displaced, and this system became completely decentralized. At the end of the century, the excise and customs taxes ceased to be used as sources of state revenue, and the decentralized property tax remained as the sole tax for state purposes.

2. *The Equalization of Tax Assessments*

The most important administrative problems that have arisen in connection with the general property tax have been in connection with its equitable assessment. When the system of assigning quotas to the towns by the supervisors was abandoned, and the assessment was thus left entirely to the local officers, it was early discovered that if the property of a town was assessed at less than its market value, the town would pay a smaller share of the state and county

[1] *Laws of* 1804, c. 94.

taxes.   The custom of undervaluation soon arose and spread rapidly, town assessors trying to outdo each other in under-assessing property within their towns.   The unfairness in the distribution of the tax resulting from this was first appre-ciated within the counties, and in 1817 [1] the board of super-visors of each county was authorized to change the total assessment of any town in the county, and thus to equalize the burden of taxation within the county.   The results of this were not always satisfactory, since in many cases a com-bination of supervisors from certain towns was formed which controlled the board and " èqualized" the assessment of towns not in the ring greatly in excess of their due propor-tion.[2]   Nevertheless, there was some improvement in county assessments; but as between the different counties there was no attempt at equalization, and the most widely varying rates of valuation developed.

The extent and effect of these unequal county valuations was, however, of comparatively little importance so long as the State tax was small, as it remained during the first half of the century.   From 1826 to 1842, indeed, there was no State tax; and from 1842 until 1850 the annual levy was always under $500,000.   In the apportionment of this amount among the various counties probably no great in-justice was caused by different rates of valuation.   But in the decade 1850–60 there was a most astonishing develop-ment in the amount of the State tax, which completely altered the situation.   In 1851, a general tax of $800,000 for schools was ordered, thus trebling at one stroke the total State tax; in 1856, the school tax was largely in-creased; during these years the tolls of the State canals were reduced, making necessary increased taxation; and

[1] *Laws of* 1817, c. 290.

[2] *Report of the Joint Committee of the Legislature,* 1863, p. 265.

larger expenditures brought about a still further increase. By 1860, the amount of the State tax was well beyond $5,000,000, having multiplied sixteen fold in ten years. Local taxation had also increased rapidly during the decade, so that the total amount of taxation had trebled within that period.[1]

The extraordinary increase in the amount of State taxation added much to the temptation to local undervaluation, and at the same time intensified greatly the inequalities resulting from varying rates of assessment. The system of uncontrolled local assessment, which had worked fairly well when taxes were small, now proved itself inadequate. The heavy burden of taxation also attracted public attention to the problem, and some remedy was demanded. The result was the creation, in 1859, of a State Board of Equalization,[2] with authority to change county assessments, similar to the authority of the supervisors to equalize town assessments.

The state board thus established consisted of six existing state officers with three State Assessors appointed by the Governor. These Assessors were required to visit every

[1] THE GENERAL PROPERTY TAX IN NEW YORK.

	Assessed Valuation.	State Taxes.	State and Local Taxes.
1846	$616,824,955	$370,557	$4,647,461
1850	727,494,583	364,003	6,312,787
1855	1,402,849,304	2,515,717	11,676,172
1860	1,419,207,520	5,440,640	18,956,024
1865	1,550,879,685	7,230,976	45,961,440
1870	1,967,001,885	14,285,976	50,328,684
1875	2,367,780,102	14,206,680	56,926,470
1880	2,637,869,238	9,232,542	49,117,782
1885	3,197,163,785	9,160,405	57,262,650
1890	3,683,653,062	8,619,748	60,493,038
1895	4,292,082,167	13,906,346	72,557,905
1897	4,506,985,694	12,033,681	80,865,704

[2] *Laws of* 1859, c. 312.

county in the State, at least once in two years, and investigate the relation of real estate assessments to valuation. From their reports the State Board of Equalization could increase or diminish the aggregate valuation of the real estate of any county, but without reducing the aggregate values of all the counties below the aggregate of the values returned by the local assessors. This statute also attempted to guard against unjust equalizations by county boards of supervisors. The supervisor of any town which considered itself aggrieved by the equalization of the board of supervisors was entitled to appeal to the State Comptroller, who was authorized, if he upheld the appeal, to make deductions from the town's share of the State tax for the following year. In 1874[1] this appellate jurisdiction over county equalizations was transferred to the State Assessors; but in practice there have been few appeals made, and little control over the local officers has been exercised through this provision.

The control of the State authority has also been limited by the absence of any power to correct individual assessments, or to compel the local assessors to change their system. The state board could act only by changing the aggregate valuation for entire counties. Along this line, however, the State Assessors and Board of Equalization have been active and energetic in the exercise of their powers. The assessors visit a number of counties each year, and in each county examine several hundred parcels of real estate, comparing the local assessment with the actual values, as evidenced by sales and the testimony of witnesses. From this evidence, the State Assessors form their opinion as to the ratio of assessed to real value in the various counties, and submit to the Board of Equalization a table of the different ratios. On this information, the state board determines the

---

[1] *Laws of* 1874, c. 351.

average rate of assessment to value for the entire State. An amount is then added to or subtracted from the assessment of each county equal to the difference between this average rate and the rate ascertained for that county. Although the board might raise the aggregate of valuations for the entire State, in practice this is never done, and whatever amount is taken from one county is added to another.

The tables of ratios presented from year to year show that while in some counties real estate is valued as high as 90 per cent. of its true value, in others it has been valued as low as 50 per cent. The state board has attempted to equalize the assessments so as to reach a uniform rate, which is usually about 65 per cent. To do this has involved considerable changes. The most striking instance is that of Westchester county, where the aggregate assessment, and consequently its proportion of the State tax, has been increased about thirty per cent. each year. In perhaps a third of the counties the increase or decrease has been more than ten per cent. of the county valuation. In the remaining two-thirds of the counties the changes indicate less glaring inequalities, and the aggregate of changes made is less than five per cent. of the aggregate assessed valuation of the entire State.

On the face of the reports of the State Assessors, it is evident that there was a considerable need for a system of equalization, and in the case of some counties the widely varying rates of assessment had produced inequalities which rendered imperative some method of adjusting the assessments of the different localities to a common basis. Nor can it be denied that the work of the State Assessors resulted to some degree in a more equitable distribution of the state tax than would be the case if there were no such central authority.

But while recognizing the need for equalization, and admitting that the work of the State Assessors secured some improvement, it was far from clear that the results of the state board's equalizations had been fully adequate in securing the fairness and equitable distribution aimed at by the law. It was urged from many sources that the State Assessors had acted unfairly, either through prejudice or with deliberate intention to lighten the burden of taxation in districts where they had special interests. Since the establishment of the State Board of Equalization such complaints have been presented by every county in the State.[1] The most persistent case is that of New York county, which has steadily protested against the increase of about $100,000,000 yearly added to the local valuations. In 1886, for example, counsel for New York appeared before the state board, submitting statements showing a lower ratio of assessment to valuation in all other counties than in New York, and claiming that for a proper equalization of the state tax, the assessment for New York county as made by the local authorities should be reduced by $271,000,000.[2] In the face of these protests, the New York county figures were increased by $112,000,000. The State Assessors asserted, as they have on other occasions,[3] that their investigations prove the ratio of assessment to valuation in New York county to be much lower than claimed, and their estimate of the ratio at 60 per cent. to be rather over than under the true situation.

In answer to the general complaints, the State Assessors admit that their equalizations do not always secure perfect results, because "no board or officials, however diligent or however conversant with the subject, can make an equalization which to themselves will be absolutely satisfactory."

---

[1] *Report of the State Assessors*, 1888, p. 11.   [2] *Ibid.*, 1886, p. 18.

[3] *Report of Tax Commissioners*, 1897, p. 19.

They do claim, however, that real estate is approximately equalized, so that all counties carry their just share, and therefore the complaints have no adequate foundation.[1]

As between the complainants and the State Assessors it is not easy to decide, but an examination and comparison of the equalization tables of the State board for a number of years throws some light on the problem. Such an investigation makes it clear that the equalizations do not in all cases show uniform tendencies, but that in many instances there are eccentric changes, which indicate, at least, that the action of the State assessors has been based on inadequate information. Thus, in 1879, the proportion of the State tax paid by Lewis, Madison and Oneida counties was suddenly reduced by a fourth, and in the following year was as suddenly raised to the former ratios. In 1889 the Cayuga county, in 1895 the Schuyler county and in 1896 the Wayne county ratios show similar variations. For Franklin county in 1894, and for Jefferson county in 1896, there were sudden temporary additions to the ratio of State tax paid. The equalized assessments for Cattaraugus county show sudden and irrational changes for every year since 1891.[2] The local assessment of Essex county (roughly, $11,000,000) has usually been reduced by $1,000,000 in the equalization

---

[1] *Report of the State Assessors,* 1888, p. 11.

[2] CATTARAUGUS COUNTY ASSESSMENTS.   (000'S OMITTED.)

YEAR.	Local Valuation.	Change by State Board.	Final Valuation.	Per cent. of State Tax Paid.
1891.	$22,973,	—$5,359,	$17,613,	.466
1892.	19,712,	—4,058,	15,563,	.399
1893.	23,105,	—2,502,	20,603,	.510
1894.	19,094,	—2,136,	16,958,	.404
1895.	22,622,	—2,582,	20,040,	.466
1896.	20,615,	—2,805,	17,810,	.408
1897.	23,508,	—3,115,	20,393,	.453

tables; but in 1892 the State Assessors, without having visited the county, added $2,500,000 to the local valuations, and the county's share of the State taxes was increased by one-third. In the following year, the county was restored to its former position among the counties which had their local assessments reduced. In 1894, the Richmond county local valuation was raised from $10,000,000 to $20,000,000; yet the State Assessors ignored the obvious increase in the rate of assessment and doubled the equalizing increment from $3,000,000 to $6,000,000.

These instances serve to show that the results of the system of equalization established in 1859 have not always been consistent; and it is clear that some of these sudden variations have been very far from the approximation to fairness claimed by the assessors. In the case of Richmond county, just mentioned, the fact that the higher valuation continued in the years following 1894 may indicate that it is not too far beyond a fair arrangement; but the rapidity of the change shows that the equalization increments before 1894 were much less than should have been added.

In addition to these defects in the operation of the system of equalizing real estate valuations, a more important problem in the administration of the general property tax arose in connection with the assessment of personal property. As early as 1859, the state comptroller called attention to the fact that not one-fifth of the taxes fell on personal property;[1] and in 1864 one of the State Assessors claimed that not one-fifth of the personalty was then reached in the assessments.[2] Since then, the personalty assessments have continued to show a large relative diminution, in the face of the well-known increase in the amount and value of property of this

[1] *Report of State Comptroller*, 1859, p. 34.

[2] *Report of Tax Commission of* 1871, p. 44.

kind. From 1860 to 1880 real estate valuations doubled, but personalty increased from $320,000,000 to only $340,-000,000. During the next decade real estate valuations were increased by $1,000,000,000 to $3,400,000,000; but personalty increased by only twelve per cent., to $382,000,-000, or one-ninth of the real estate. The census estimate of the value of tangible personal property in New York State in 1890 was $2,700,000,000, more than seven times the assessed valuation of all personalty. After 1890, there appeared a slight tendency to an increase in personalty valuations, but by 1896 the total for the state was only $544,000,000, or less than one-seventh of the real estate valuation.

Proposals to remedy these conditions by means of a more thorough central control over the local assessors were frequently made. The celebrated Tax Commission of 1871 asserted that "The fault [in ill-adjusted and unfair valuations] is not in the statute, but its administration. The remedy, therefore, must be found in making the administration more effective or in compelling the assessors to do their duty in accordance with the strict meaning and provisions of the statute. And this, in the opinion of the commissioners, can only be effected by the creation of some central authority . . . who, clothed with all proper authority and supported by the law officers of the State should be required to practically enforce the laws. . . . As it is now, the system has no recognized head or central spirit of authority, whose sole province is to secure alike the enforcement of the laws and to learn by experience and investigation how best to remedy their imperfections."[1] The State Assessors, in 1877, urged the establishment of a State department of assessment and taxation, with power to make rules and regulations for

[1] *Report of Tax Commission*, 1871, p. 48.

the government and control of local assessors, and to remove them for incompetency, neglect of duty, and violations of the rules and regulations of the department. One of the assessors, in 1879, advocated an increase in the number of State Assessors to nine, in order to allow of more accurate examinations and a better knowledge of local conditions.

There is no evidence of any recognition by the legislature of any of these recommendations, and the powers of the State authorities remained unaltered. The Tax Commission of 1880 seem to have failed to recognize any need for strengthening the hands of the State Assessors, but the counsel appointed by the Governor in 1892 to revise the tax laws strongly urged that " a thorough and complete supervision by a competent and authorized board will, to a very great extent, by an energetic administration of the present laws, prevent very many of the existing abuses, and result in the enforcement of very salutary provisions now neglected or ignored." [1] The specific recommendations made at this time were that the number of State Assessors should be increased to five, who with the State Comptroller should constitute a board of Tax Commissioners for the supervision of all assessments and matters of taxation. At the meetings of the county equalizing boards a State Assessor should be present to make the decision in case of disagreement between the town assessors and supervisors; the right of appeal to the state board being also granted. [2]

The first legislation along the lines of these recommendations was enacted in the revised Tax Law of 1896. [3] The State Assessors were replaced by three Tax Commissioners appointed by the Governor, to whom were given, in addition to the former powers of the State Assessors, authority:

---

[1] *Report of Counsel*, 1893, p. 12.   [2] *Ibid.*, 1893, p. 18, 89.

[3] *Laws of* 1896, c. 908.

"To investigate and examine methods of assessment within the State."

"To furnish local assessors with information to aid them in making assessments."

"To make rules and regulations to enforce these provisions."

"To ascertain whether the assessors faithfully discharged their duties, and particularly as to their compliance with this act requiring the assessment of all property not exempt from taxation at its full value."

This law thus authorized a more thorough supervision and control over the local assessors; but it will be noticed that in two important particulars it fell short of the recommendations already cited. In the first place, there was no increase in the number of state officers, so as to make possible a more extended and more careful comparison of local values with assessments on which to base a more accurate adjustment of equalizations. Secondly, the tax commissioners were given no authority over individual assessments, and the decisions of local assessors, in this respect, remained subject to no revision by a higher authority.

The additional authority provided by the new law has, however, secured some tangible results. Acting on the powers conferred, the tax commissioners during the year 1897 issued instructions to the local assessors insisting that all property must be assessed at its true value, and threatening to prosecute any local board of assessors that failed to make an honest assessment. This pressure on the local assessors secured a large increase in the assessment in some counties. In seven counties the increase in real estate valuations was more than 50 per cent. over the figures for the previous year; in Herkimer county the increase was $10,-000,000, or 70 per cent.; in Westchester county $73,000,000, or 78 per cent.; and in Suffolk county $26,000,000, or 137 per cent. In most of the counties where real estate valuations had been at a low rate, as shown in the equalization tables, the assessment rate was raised to a point much nearer the average rate for the entire state. This average rate, however, is still much below the true value, and there are yet many variations between the rates in different counties. Moreover, local equalizations by the county supervisors continued in many cases to increase rather than diminish the injustice of varying rates of valuation.[1]

A more significant change secured was the increase in personalty assessments. In twenty-eight counties there was an increase of over 50 per cent. and in thirteen counties of over 100 per cent. In Richmond county the increase was from $115,000 to $1,628,000; and in Westchester county from $4,000,000 to $24,000,000. For the entire State, the increase on personalty was $105,000,000, nearly twenty per cent. over the figures for 1896.[2] But, "the enforcement of the law resulting in such increase has, in many instances, caused added injustice to rural communities, where the burden of taxation has hitherto fallen most heavily."[3] New York county had shown almost no increase in personalty valuations, and the other counties containing large cities, where personalty has been most undervalued, have a much smaller increase than the rural counties. The total assessment for personalty is yet only a seventh of the real estate assessments; and the Tax Commissioners consider it manifest that the operation of the law as regards the taxation of personalty is still a practical failure.

The Tax Commissioners, taking warning from the failure of earlier proposals for radical changes, have not advocated any further additions to their power; but they have recom-

---

[1] *Report of the Tax Commissioners*, 1897, p. 9.

[2] *Ibid.*, 1897, p. 32.   [3] *Ibid.*, p. 3.

mended and secured from the legislature of 1898 a reorganization of the system of county equalizations. Under this plan the equalizations of the different towns in each county are to be made not by the board of supervisors, but by three commissioners appointed by the supervisors for the purpose. These commissioners are required to make careful examinations of the conditions in the different towns, and their equalizations should thus be based on more accurate information than was possible under the supervisor system.

The operation of this law and further experience under the law of 1896 may secure a more equitable apportionment of the general property tax. If, however, serious inequalities continue, there remain but two possible remedies. The general property tax may be abandoned as a state tax. Already a large part of the State income is from other sources, and it would not be impossible to rearrange the system so as to secure all the revenue for the State from these, and leave the general property tax as a purely local tax.[1] The other alternative is to accept the proposals for further centralization. The steps already taken in that direction have produced some improvement in the situation, and a more thorough central control might secure still better results.

3. *Administration of New State Taxes*

The revenue of New York State is to-day derived in large part from other sources than the general property tax. In 1880, the tax on corporations was established; in 1885, the inheritance tax; and, in 1896, the excise tax became once more in part a source of state revenue. From these taxes the State receives annually over $8,000,000, more than two-thirds the amount received from the State property tax.

[1] This has been advocated by the present State Comptroller, in his *Report*, 1898, pp. 12–20.

The administrative arrangements for the assessment and collection of these new taxes show examples both of centralization and of central control over local officials. The corporation tax has been from the first assessed and collected solely by the officers of the State Comptroller's department; the inheritance tax is administered by local officials, but subject to a limited amount of central direction and supervision by the State Comptroller; and in the new excise tax both methods are employed. A consideration of the system of administration for each of these taxes is, therefore, of interest to our subject.

The Corporation Tax. Under the corporation tax law of 1880,[1] the president or treasurer of corporations subject to the tax was required to report to the comptroller, making statements under oath of the valuation of capital stock, of dividends, premiums or gross receipts, as the case might be for different sorts of corporations. The assessment of the tax was to be made by the comptroller practically on these valuations furnished by the corporation officers, since no means were provided to enable him to correct their statements.

The administrative machinery thus provided for the execution of the corporation tax law does not seem to have been adopted as the result of any conscious and deliberate policy of centralization; but rather arose from the nature of the large railroad and insurance companies from whom the bulk of the tax must be collected. The activities of these corporations reaching far beyond the limits of any local administrative district, it was almost self-evident that the only practicable valuation was on the business throughout the whole of the state, and that the simplest form of collection was by a single payment direct to the state treasury. Moreover, although the administration was centralized in form,

---

[1] *Laws of* 1880, c. 542.

there was no important increase in the number of State administrative officials.   There was not even any machinery provided by which the Comptroller could secure a list of all the corporations subject to the tax, and the additional duties imposed on the Comptroller were almost purely clerical, and conferred little increase of real authority.

An amendment to the tax law in 1882[1] authorized the Comptroller to appoint commissioners to examine the books and records of any corporation, in order to determine the amount of the tax due from it; but the lack of an appropriation prevented this provision from going into effect, and the enforcement of the law continued for ten years longer in the hands of the corporations themselves.   In 1892, the Comptroller called the attention of the legislature to the fact that this method of administration involved a serious loss to the state treasury, and stated emphatically that there was "not sufficient authority provided for this department to determine the amout of the tax fairly due, or to make proper examinations and investigations, and enforce liability."[2] This secured the necessary appropriation, and the law of 1882 was then acted on by the appointment of a commissioner to examine the accounts of corporations in New York City, and in the following year a second commissioner was appointed with headquarters at Buffalo.   The result of their examinations, in which the attendance of witnesses and production of book accounts and vouchers were compelled, enabled the Comptroller to secure the facts necessary for a true valuation.

The list of corporations paying the tax, however, remained largely incomplete.   The great transportation, telegraph, telephone and lighting companies were shining marks and had soon appeared on the Comptroller's records; but many

---

[1] *Laws of* 1882, c. 151.   [2] *Comptroller's Report*, 1892, p. 23.

of the smaller corporations avoided the tax. In 1894 Comptroller Roberts secured an appropriation to carry on an investigation of the records in the offices of the Secretary of State and the county clerks, for the purpose of ascertaining and taxing the delinquent corporations. In two years, the number of corporations paying the tax was doubled, and more than half a million dollars was added to the State's income from these newly added corporations.[1] A continuation of the work further increased the number of corporations and the annual revenue from the corporation tax. The force employed in making these investigations is, however, only temporary, as it is expected when a complete list of existing corporations is secured that reports from the Secretary of State to the Comptroller of new certificates of incorporation issued will enable the list to be kept complete. The permanent administrative force employed in the administration of the corporation tax law is thus insignificant, and apart from the two commissioners in New York and Buffalo, consists of clerks in the Comptroller's office at Albany.

The original assessment for the corporation tax may be reviewed and altered on the claim of any corporation for a reduction, after a rehearing had before the Comptroller or his deputy. Appeals from the Comptroller's final valuations now follow the usual American course in being taken to a judicial and not to an administrative authority. Under the original law the State Board of Equalization decided on such appeals, and by law of 1882 the Secretary of State, Attorney General and State Treasurer were made the appellate authority; but since 1889 the remedy has been by writ of certiorari before the Supreme Court, from whose decision either party may carry the question to the Court of Appeals.[2]

The compulsory collection of the tax where payment is

---

[1] *Comptroller's Report*, 1896, p. 8.   [2] *Laws of* 1889, c. 463.

refused is accomplished by the sheriffs of the counties acting under instructions from the Comptroller; and the warrant of the Comptroller commanding the sheriff to levy on the real and personal property of the delinquent must be acted on by that officer in the same manner as a warrant issued upon a judgment of a court of record. In this feature of the law we have a significant instance of a central administrative power of direction over local officials.

The Inheritance Tax. The assessment and collection of the Inheritance Tax could not, like the Corporation Tax, be attended to directly from the State Comptroller's office. A system of local officials to appraise and value the property to be taxed is necessary, and the collection of the tax can be facilitated by the use of local agents. A machinery of local subordinates to the Comptroller's department might have been created for this purpose; but in fact the local administration of this tax was turned over to already existing local officials. Appraisers are appointed by the surrogate of the county, since that officer is in charge of the probate of wills and grants letters of administration, and thus receives notice of any decease where property is left. On the appraiser's report, the surrogate determines the value of the property and the amount of the tax. Payment is made to the county treasurer, who remits the amount to the State Treasurer; and in cases of failure to pay the tax the county treasurer notifies the district attorney to prosecute the delinquents in the surrogate's court.

It was perhaps natural that these new duties placed on local officials by a general law without providing any central supervision or direction, should not at first be thoroughly performed, but there is also evidence that these local officials were openly negligent. Comptroller Campbell says that "for several years after the passage of the Act of 1885 it received only a negative support from local officers. Estates were settled in surrogates' courts and the funds distributed without any inquiry being made as to whether there was a tax due the State thereon.   County treasurers received such sums as were paid to them voluntarily by executors or administrators, without knowing or taking any steps to ascertain whether the amount of the tax had been fixed and determined as required by law.   The methods pursued were extremely lax ; the law was evaded and violated with apparent impunity, and the State deprived of a large amount of revenue to which it was. entitled."[1]

When the collateral inheritance tax was transformed to a tax on all inheritances by the transfer tax law of 1892,[2] the administration of the tax was better provided for.   The new law entered into more cumbersome and complicated details as to the duties of local officers, required them to use blank forms provided by the Comptroller, and directed the surrogates to make regular reports to that officer of applications for letters of administration on estates, the amounts of legacies, deeds and conveyances, the proceedings to determine the amounts of the taxes, and the amounts assessed. These provisions gave the Comptroller a certain power of control over the surrogates and county treasurers.   At the same time, an appropriation for assistants to the Comptroller made possible an investigation of the records in the surrogates' offices.   These measures secured a more effective enforcement of the law, evidenced by the disappearance from the Comptroller's reports of the former complaints of negligence on the part of local officials.   There was also a striking increase in the revenue derived from the tax; and although part of this was due to the change in the tax, in part it was the result of the change in administrative methods strengthening the Comptroller's authority.[3]

[1] *Comptroller's Report*, 1893, p. 23.   [2] *Laws of* 1892, c. 399.

[3] *Comptroller's Report*, 1894, p. 24.

The central control established in 1892 had removed the most striking deficiencies of the former system; but only to reveal the possibility of securing still greater efficiency by further increasing the power of the Comptroller. The locally appointed appraisers seem to be in many cases subject to local influence in making their valuations, and make reports which do not give the State the full amount of the tax it should receive. Comptroller Roberts has urged that as the inheritance tax is a State tax for the collection of which the Comptroller is nominally responsible, he should be authorized to appoint appraisers, at least for the important counties.[1]

The legislature has not so far seen fit thus to centralize the assessment of the inheritance tax; but to avoid undervaluations has provided under certain conditions for a reappraisal of estates subject to the tax. Under laws of 1896 and 1897,[2] a copy of every appraiser's report must be filed with the State Comptroller, and if he is dissatisfied with the assessment he may apply to a justice of the Supreme Court of the district to appoint an appraiser to revalue the estates. On the report of an appraiser so appointed the justice may make a new determination of the amount of the tax. The power of initiative here conferred on the Comptroller gives him a limited power over the surrogates: but the effective control established is that of the justices of the Supreme Court.

It is interesting to note here the imposition of administrative functions on judicial officers in the execution of the inheritance tax law. The duties assigned to the surrogates under the law are a clear departure from the idea of the separation of judicial from administrative functions. Under

---

[1] *Comptroller's Report*, 1895, p. 18.

[2] *Laws of* 1896, c. 908; *ibid.*, 1897, c. 248.

these more recent amendments the Supreme Court justices are made to act first as an administrative court in deciding on the appeal of the Comptroller, and then in a purely administrative capacity in appointing the appraiser and in fixing the amount of the tax.

Another complaint made by the Comptroller has been that the allowances made by the surrogates to the appraisers are in some counties far in excess of the value of any service rendered. In one county the fees have been about forty per cent. of the tax collected.[1] In 1895, the Comptroller asked for legislative authority to audit appraisers accounts before they had been allowed; but no action was taken. The following year the department ruled that it already possessed this power under section 3295 of the Code of Civil procedure, which provides that "when the fees or other charges of an officer are chargeable to the State, they must be audited by the Comptroller and paid on his warrant, except as otherwise specially prescribed by law."

The Comptroller's power of control in the assessment of the inheritance tax is thus exercised by means of the reports required from the appraisers and surrogates, by examinations of county records, through the power of appealing to the Supreme Court justices for a re-appraisal, and by this audit of the accounts of appraisers. It is even yet a very limited authority, and if it is sufficient to secure efficiency in the administration of the law, it illustrates the great extent to which decentralization may be safely allowed in this country.

The Liquor Tax. The history of excise legislation during the century and a quarter in which the revenues received from the liquor traffic went solely to local treasuries, and the administration was in the hands of local officials, does not concern our present subject. The only attempt to control

---

[1] *Comptroller's Report*, 1896, p. 14.

the administration of the liquor laws by the State officials was under the law of 1866, providing that the board of health for the Metropolitan Sanitary District (the members of which were appointed by the Governor) should be the board of excise within the same district. This however proved only temporary, as with the charter of 1870[1] the local officials were again placed in control.

Until 1870 the general system of administering the excise laws outside of the cities was determined by the law of 1857,[2] which was in the main a re-enactment of the system in force before the prohibition law of 1855. Three commissioners of excise were appointed in each county by the county judge and two justices of the peace; these commissioners granted licenses under the provisions of the statutes. In 1870[3] this county system was changed to a system of town boards, and in 1873 a system of local prohibition at the option of any town was provided for.[4] Before the passage of the law of 1896, there were 925 town, 2 village and 37 city boards of excise.

The changes made by the statute of 1896[5] were radical in their nature. Instead of licenses issued in the discretion of local authorities, the liquor traffic was made free to all persons who should pay the required tax; the amount of this tax varied with the population of different localities, but was much higher than the former license fees; one-third of the revenue was reserved for the State treasury; the system of local option was extended by providing several alternative schemes of partial and complete prohibition; and finally, the administrative machinery, with which we are here especially concerned, was completely altered,

---

[1] *Laws of* 1870, c. 137.   [2] *Ibid.*, 1857, c. 628.   [3] *Ibid.*, 1870, c. 175.

[4] *Ibid.*, 1873, c. 549, § 6.   People *v.* Excise Commissioners of Randolph, 75 *Hun's Reports*, p. 224.

[5] *Ibid.*, 1896, c. 112.

both in form and in its relations to the State government. Existing town and city boards of excise were abolished, and the collection of the liquor taxes was transferred from town and city officers to county treasurers, who were also charged with the distribution of the revenue between the State and towns and cities.   Still further, there was created a State department of excise, with a corps of State officers to exercise supervision over the local officers, to investigate the enforcement of the statute, and in New York, Kings and Erie counties to administer the law in every respect.

At the head of the department was placed the State Commissioner of Excise, appointed by the Governor for a term of five years at a salary of $5,000 per annum.   In each county containing a city of the first class the State Commissioner appoints a special deputy commissioner to collect and distribute the liquor taxes in these counties.   For the supervision of these deputy commissioners and the county treasurers in other counties, these officers are required to use books of record and account and forms of bonds and tax certificates provided and directed by the State Commissioner, and to make such reports and exhibit such records as the State Commissioner shall require.   At the same time it is made the duty of the State Commissioner to "cause the accounts and vouchers of all excise moneys collected and paid over to the State and to the several localities by each county treasurer and special deputy commissioner of excise in the State, and the records of all transactions by them under the liquor tax law to be carefully examined, and the result of such examination certified to the State Comptroller at least once in every year."   To make effective this supervision by means of audit of accounts and examination of records, and for other purposes, the State Commissioner of Excise is directed to appoint not more than sixty special agents to "investigate all matters relating to the collection of liquor

taxes and penalties under this act and in relation to the
compliance with law by persons engaged in the traffic in
liquors."

The actual enforcement of the law through criminal prosecutions still depends mainly on the local courts. Actions
for imposing the penalties in the act must be handled by
district attorneys, and must go through the regular channels
of local grand and petit juries. It is, however, the duty of
the special deputies and special agents (as well as the county
treasurers, sheriffs and police officers) to notify the district
attorney of any violation of the law. By thus furnishing a
large amount of material evidence their investigations aid in
securing the enforcement of the law; but if a district attorney
neglects or refuses to perform his duty, the only remedy is
to prefer charges to the Governor, who, on examination, may
remove him from office. In two respects, however, a more
direct authority is given to the State Excise officials to secure enforcement of the law. Where any person unlawfully
traffics in liquor without obtaining a liquor tax certificate, or
contrary to any provision of the act, the State Commissioner
or any of his subordinates may apply to a justice of the
Supreme Court of the judicial district for an order enjoining
the traffic in liquor by the person charged. If the injunc-
tion is issued, its violation is deemed a contempt of court
and punishable accordingly. The State Commissioner of
Excise may also bring a civil action in any court of record
for the recovery of any penalty imposed for a violation of
the liquor tax law;[1] this authority being conferred for use
where the local authorities cannot or will not do their
duties. The State Commissioner is further authorized to appoint attorneys to act with any special deputy or special
agent in the prosecution of any action or proceeding brought

---

[1] *Laws of* 1897, c. 312.

under the provisions of the Liquor Tax Act or the acts repealed by it.

The State excise department by these various provisions has an effective control over the collection of the excise revenue; its officials serve to aid the local officers in the enforcement of the penal provisions of the law; and in cases where local officers do not act vigorously, the State department has a limited power of direct enforcement by means of civil actions and applications for injunctions.

A discussion of centralization in administration is not concerned with the questions of public policy that have been raised in connection with the new liquor law. The wisdom of using this source of revenue for state purposes, and the relative advantages of the tax system and other systems of controlling the liquor traffic are alike beyond the scope of this inquiry. Whatever may be the decision on these points, from the purely administrative point of view the operation of the more centralized system during its past two years has given satisfactory results. The excise revenue of $12,000,-000 a year has been collected under the new arrangements for the same expense as the former revenue of $3,000,000 a year. The examination of the county treasurer's accounts, besides guarding the state against loss of revenue, has promoted uniformity of system and has been of much help to the local officials in their work.[1] As a result of the work of the special agents the number of those illegally trafficking in liquor has been greatly reduced.[2] Formerly, in certain localities, liquor was sold without license as openly as other merchandise, some localities going so far as to refuse or neglect to elect the boards of excise provided for in the old law.

The results of criminal prosecutions which are not subject

---

[1] *Excise Commissioner's Reports*, i, 22; ii, 25.   [2] *Ibid.*, ii, 7.

to active central control are much as they have always been. " In localities where there is a healthy public sentiment in favor of law and order, convictions for violations of excise laws are common. In other places, where public sentiment is indifferent or hostile to the execution of any law regulating the liquor trade, and where jurors and other public officials are selected with reference to protection rather than punishment of violators, few, if any, convictions occur or can be expected."[1] The court proceedings instituted by the state department have been of some effect. Eleven proceedings were instituted to restrain illegal traffic in liquor, which secured the issue of injunctions in eight cases. Twenty-two proceedings were commenced by the department, and fifty actions by citizens to revoke and cancel liquor tax certificates, which resulted in orders revoking and cancelling 36 certificates, 26 cases were dismissed or discontinued and 13 were still pending.[2] This indicates that the authority of the state department to initiate proceedings in the courts has been of considerable effect in securing obedience to the law.

The exercise of State control over the collection of any part of the State revenue would not be inconsistent with the widest extension of local self-government. The New York liquor tax, however, while partly a State tax, goes in large part to the local treasuries of the towns and cities. It is therefore of interest to note that the Court of Appeals in sustaining the law has declared emphatically that excise administration in this State has always been a State function, and that even the officials who executed the former laws were acting not as local but as State officers. The former excise commissioners, says the court, "although locally elected, were State agencies for administering the excise system. . . . In granting licenses they were not exercising

---

[1] *Excise Commissioner's Report*, ii, 11.   [2] *Ibid.*, ii, 20.

a jurisdiction as agents of the corporation within which they
acted, for the granting of licenses for the traffic in liquor was
not a power vested in towns, villages or cities. They exercised their functions under the authority of the State, which
prescribed their powers and duties, and the mode of their
appointment was a convenient method for designating the
agencies through which the system should be administered.
. . . . The granting of licenses for the liquor traffic has
never been a corporate function or duty of a city as such.
It is a function which the State in its aggregate capacity has
administered. It has made use of local machinery, ...
and it has permitted the cities to use excise moneys for local
purposes. But excise laws do not relate to the affairs of
cities."[1]

This position is also indicated in earlier opinions on
closely related questions;[2] and the decision upholding the
State control over excise administration on this ground is
significant in view of the many other functions performed by
city officials which are likewise not of a corporate character
but are duties of State administration. Over all such matters in which the city officials act as agents of the State, a
similar central control might be established.

4. *Central Control over Local Finance*

The first act defining the duties of the State Comptroller
authorized him " to audit, liquidate and settle all accounts
. . . between this State, and any person acting or having
acted under the authority of the same." [3] This comprehensive provision would seem to have authorized a central

---

[1] 149 *New York Reports*, p. 375.

[2] Lorrillard *v.* Town of Monroe, 11 *New York Reports*, p. 392; People *v.* Board
of Town Auditors, 74 *New York Reports*, p. 310.

[3] *Laws of* 1782, c. 21.

audit of all county and city treasurers' accounts so far as
they were concerned with the collection of State revenues.
In practice, however, no such control was ever exercised
under this provision, and it is only within recent years that
a limited amount of control over county treasurers, through
central audit of some of their accounts, has come to be
established.   Attention has already been called to the audit
by the Comptroller over the accounts for the inheritance
tax, and by the Excise Commissioner over accounts for the
liquor tax.   In addition, the Comptroller has the power of
auditing the Court and Trust Fund accounts of the county
treasurers.   This power was conferred by certain amendments to the Code of Civil Procedure, made in 1892, transferring the supervision of the Court and Trust Funds in the
hands of the various county treasurers from the various
courts to the State Comptroller.[1]   That official is directed to
" prescribe regulations and rules for the care and disposition
thereof, which shall be observed by all parties interested
therein, unless the court having jurisdiction over the same
shall make different directions by special orders."   He is
also required to name depositories for such funds, and at
least once in each year to cause an examination to be made
of the accounts of the officials having the custody of these
funds, and is authorized to employ special clerks for this
purpose.

   The introduction of this system soon disclosed the fact
that there had been no uniform method pursued by county
treasurers in keeping such funds, and in many instances no
separate account had been kept of different funds, but all
were bunched together in almost inextricable confusion.[2]
These accounts were straightened out, a uniform system of

[1] *Laws of* 1892, c. 651;   *Code of Civil Procedure,* § 744.

[2] *Comptroller's Reports,* 1894, p. 13;   1895, p. 30.

book-keeping introduced, and rules formulated for the administration of these funds. By means of these arrangements and examinations, deficits and defalcations in these accounts are made more difficult, and if made are discovered in time to prevent loss, whereas under the former system it was sometimes years after the defalcation before discovery was made. Inquiries showed that within recent years defalcations or shortages had taken place in thirty-three counties. This condition of affairs naturally has led to the suggestion that the system of examination by a State authority now established for court and trust funds, the collateral inheritance tax and excise accounts, be extended to include all the county treasurers' accounts.[1] No action has, however, been taken as yet on this suggestion.

City finances are now subject to external control only through the constitutional limitations on the total amount of city debt and the city tax rate. But formerly they were limited by a legislative control over the taxing power, which in the case of New York city was used at one period to actively control the city's expenditures. The historical explanation of this legislative control lies in the fact that the early municipal charters, following the precedents of English borough charters, conferred on the municipal corporations no power of taxation. When the colonial legislatures authorized the cities to levy taxes, those were at first only for limited amounts necessary for specific purposes,[2] and the tax laws had to be repeated from year to year. Early in this century, however, these special laws gave way to general authorizations, and new city charters conferred on the municipal corporations the authority to levy taxes. But for New York city the practice of passing annual tax

---

[1] *Comptroller's Reports*, 1896, p. 451; 1897, p. 51.

[2] *Colonial Laws of New York*, 1691, c. 18; 1701, c. 96; 1724, c. 454; 1753, c. 941; 1764, c. 1259; c. 1261.

laws was continued, though up to the middle of the century the action of the legislature was merely formal. The laws did not prescribe the details of the city budget, and little if any change was made in the bills submitted by the city for approval.[1]

The period of active legislative control over New York city finances is closely connected with changes in the organization of the city government which took place at the same time. As early as 1844 the board of education was given authority to determine the amount of the expenditure for schools,[2] and the council ceased to have any control over this item. In 1849 the department of charities and correction was also placed under an elected board,[3] which determined the amount of taxes necessary for its use independently of the council. These changes, while weakening the financial responsibility of the council, did not establish any central control. The first step in that direction is seen in the city tax law of 1851,[4] which, for the first time, named in detail the items for which the tax should be levied; but as no change was made in the appropriations voted by the city authorities, no effective control was yet established. In 1856, however, the legislative committee took testimony of witnesses and made changes in ten items, reducing the total levy authorized for general purposes from \$3,485,944 to \$3,247,189. The next year important changes were made in the city organization. A separate board of county supervisors was provided, elected by a system of minority representation which gave the minority party half of the board. This board was to have entire charge of all county expenditures. At the same time a State Park Commission and a

---

[1] E. D. Durand, *The Finances of New York City*, p. 27. The account of legislative control over New York City finances is based on the facts in ch. iv. of Mr. Durand's book.

[2] *Laws of* 1844, c. 320.   [3] *Ibid.*, 1849, c. 246.   [4] *Ibid.*, 1851, c. 258.

State Metropolitan Police Board[1] were established, supplanting the city departments. Later, State commissions were appointed in place of the city fire, health and excise departments.[2] The creation of these independent departments subtracted much from the authority of the city council, and that body undertook to limit their activity by refusing appropriations. This only led to further legislative action. Additional amounts were inserted in the city tax bill by the legislature for these neglected items, and the mayor and comptroller were directed to order the payments. At the same time, the legislature regularly cut down the items voted by the council, and by laws against transferring balances from one account to another, and forbidding the payment of a judgment for an amount more than the appropriation, prevented the council from evading the legislative control. During the 60's practically the entire appropriating power for the city came to be exercised directly by the legislature.[3]

The loose financial methods and the flagrant corruption of the local authorities at this period form a strong justification for a strict central control over the city's finances; and one needs only to recall the gigantic frauds of the Tweed regime to recognize the need for some effective check to such management. During the period that the central control was a real

---

[1] *Laws of* 1857, c. 569, c. 771.   [2] *Ibid.*, 1865, c. 249; *Ibid.*, 1866, c. 74.

[3] The comparatively small field in which the council had any control over expenditures is indicated by the following table of estimated appropriations for 1868 (from E. D. Durand, *op. cit.*, p. 87):

State taxes	$5,564,426
State commissions	4,151,519
Other independent departments	4,755,493
County expenditures	3,263,758
Interest and debt redemption	1,847,111
Under control of council	3,710,709
Total	$23,293,016

force it seems clear that it wrought a considerable improvement. The city departments under the State commissions seem to have been free from the corruption which prevailed in the departments under the rule of the city authorities; and the legislative control over the city taxes seems to have been some check through its reductions in items approved by the councils. But legislative control did not prove a thoroughly effective check. The motive for its establishment had been largely partisan, due to the political conditions in the city and State before and during the war time. Hence partisan motives played a large part in the changes made by the legislature. Further, the careful consideration by practised experts necessary to an efficient control could not be given by either the legislature or its committees, and the city tax laws were regularly rushed through, sometimes at the end of the session without reading. After a time the city ring obtained control of the legislature, which then in place of a restraining influence became a powerful tool in the hands of the very men whose acts it was necessary to control. Finally, by the charter of 1870, the independent departments were restored to the city, and the legislature abandoned its supervision over the city appropriations.

It is of interest here to notice a proposal made to the Constitutional Convention of 1867 by Professor Francis Lieber, of Columbia College, that city comptrollers should be appointed by the legislature, or by the governor, with a proper inspection over them.[1] Such a system of central administrative control through the auditing of all city bills would have provided a more effective means of detecting fraud than was possible under the system of legislative control; and it would have done so without interfering with the actual administration of the city affairs by the local

---

[1] F. Lieber, *Changes proposed in the Constitution of New York* (1867), p. 84.

officials.   No action was, however, taken on the suggestion, and the idea seems to have been entirely forgotten for a quarter of a century.

A more recent plan to establish a central administrative supervision over municipal accounts was the bill proposed in 1891 by the Fassett Committee on cities, requiring each city to file annually with the State Comptroller a report of the financial administration of the preceding year.[1]   These reports were to be made on blank forms furnished by the State Comptroller, who could prepare summary tables for submission to the legislature.   This proposal, though far short of the scheme for a central audit of city accounts, would have compelled all the cities in the State to adopt the same general system of book-keeping and titles of accounts. It would thus have made public the facts relating to municipal conditions on a uniform basis, which would make possible accurate and definite comparisons of the results in different cities.   Such comparative statements would furnish a basis for intelligent local criticism of the work of any particular city government, would make the practical experience of each city available for all the others, and would present information essential to wise and careful legislation on the question of municipal government.   Nevertheless the bill proposed by the committee failed of adoption.

Five years later another and somewhat broader scheme of central administrative control over cities was proposed by the commissions appointed to frame uniform charters for cities of the second and third classes in New York.   These commissions recommended the creation of a State Municipal Government Board, the members to be appointed by the Governor, which should have a general supervision over all cities of the second and third classes (which include all the

---

[1] *Fassett Committee Report*, v, 22.

cities in the State with less than 250,000 inhabitants). To
this end it was proposed that this board should have authority: (1) to prescribe uniform methods of book-keeping
and of keeping statistics, and a form of report for every
municipal department; (2) to pass upon the regularity of
all municipal bond issues before they are placed on the
market; and (3) to act as a permanent committee to consider and report to the legislature on all bills relating to the
cities under its supervision.[1]   This proposal, like that of the
Fassett committee, has failed of adoption; it was not even
debated in the legislature of 1896, and the uniform charter
for cities of the second class, passed in 1898, contains no
reference to a state board of control.

[1] F. W. Holls, *State Boards of Municipal Control*, in *Report of Baltimore
Conference on Good City Government*, p. 226. See also, for a discussion on
central administrative control over cities, F. J. Goodnow, *Municipal Problems*,
ch. iv.

CHAPTER VI

CONCLUSION

WE have now studied the various fields of administration which show a tendency towards centralization. In each case the conditions existing at the time of the passage of the centralizing measures have been noticed; the results of these measures, as tested by the standard of efficiency, have been pointed out; and some further advances in the same direction have been suggested. These explanations, tests and suggestions, however, apply only to each particular department of governmental action; and, in view of the many fields in which some tendency toward centralization has appeared, it becomes important to seek more general and more fundamental causes, and to consider the principles of a sound and consistent administrative policy suited to present and prospective conditions. In practice, we have drifted away from former theories of administration; it is now time to take our bearings and to lay out a definite course for the future.

The administrative centralization that has developed in New York may be ascribed in part to the social ideals of a democracy. It is true that any form of state action or central control is an impairment of the independent self-government of the local districts. But local self-government is only one form of democracy; in the State and nation democracy is, not the government, but the popular sovereignty behind the representative government. It is this popular sovereignty in the larger communities which in striving after its social ideals has proved a centralizing force in many fields, and among them in the field of state government. Universal suffrage requires a system of popular education in order that the franchise may be exercised with intelligence. The higher conception of manhood which gives rise to and which results from universal suffrage develops a demand for more humane treatment of the poor, of the disabled and even of the convicted criminal. To secure the attainment of these democratic aims it has been necessary to limit the independence of the town or county by establishing central control or by providing for direct State administration.

In the practical realization of these ideals, much is due to other causes. More especially, economic changes have made easy their fulfillment, and have also produced conditions which of themselves go far to account for much of the centralization of state administration.

The transformation of New York State from a collection of small farming communities with a total population of 340,000, to a thickly populated area of 7,000,000 people, most of them living in cities and engaged in manufacturing and commercial pursuits would seem to necessitate important changes in political institutions. We have already noticed how this growth and concentration of population brings about *ipso facto* the phenomenon of local centralization.[1] The same factors also produce conditions that call for extensions of direct state administration and a state control over local officials. The increase of population involves a corresponding increase in the number of school children; it has involved also a more than proportionate increase in the number of the dependent, defective and criminal classes; and the concentration of population has made necessary a vast

[1] See p. 16.

deal of sanitary regulation over matters which in a rural community needs no regulation whatever. This increase of work to be done of itself makes necessary a more complex organization. It also gives opportunity for more complete classification through the use of state institutions. This, then, offers a general explanation for state control in education, charities, correction and health; and for the establishment of state normal schools, hospitals and prisons.

The increase of wealth, which has been even more rapid than the increase of population, has also been an important cause in the development of administrative centralization. The great development of State taxation, which accentuated the inequalities of local assessments and led to central control, was made possible only by the increase of wealth to be taxed. The appearance of new forms of wealth which easily escaped the general property tax led to the establishment of the new forms of taxation, in which direct State administration or a central control was almost inevitable. Through the concentration of wealth in certain localities, a State tax became a means by which the richer communities could be brought to contribute to the poorer. The State school tax and State tax for the care of the insane thus gave to the rural districts more than the amount raised in such districts by the State tax; and the State grant being thus, not simply apparent, but a positive contribution, central control over the schools and State care of the insane have been more readily accepted.

In the third place, the revolution in the means and conditions of transportation has opened the way to centralizing influences. Central control of local officials under the conditions of communication existing before the middle of the century would necessarily have been exercised without any adequate knowledge of the local situation. In the stage-coach period traveling was too expensive and occupied too

much time to permit any efficient central inspection of local
conditions; and without this inspection central control was
likely to do more harm than good. Under these circumstances the advantages of local independence were decisive.
With the transportation conditions of to-day, however, not
only is the actual outlay for traveling expenses much less
(considering the decline in the importance of a unit of
money, it is enormously less), but the time occupied in
passing from one place to another has been reduced from
days to hours. It is possible now for a few officials to make
local examinations over a wide reach of territory, traveling
in comfort and without spending more time *en route* than in
making inspections. Further, easy and rapid communication by post and telegraph make possible elaborate systems
of reports, which furnish to the central offices prompt and
accurate knowledge of local conditions, on the basis of which
central action can be wisely undertaken.

In addition to the traceable effects of increased population,
increased wealth and easier means of communication, there
would seem to be some connection between the general stage
of economic development and the character of political institutions. As late as sixty years ago, industry in the United
States was almost wholly confined to agriculture, each local
community was largely self-sustaining, and the unit of all
economic action was the individual or the family. Under
these conditions of local independence in economic activities,
it was natural that a similar independence should be found
in all fields of action, and that theories and ideals of the best
methods of political action should be affected by the actual
practice of the times. But since then economic conditions
and relations have been entirely revolutionized. In place of
self-sustaining towns, there is a larger and larger amount of
local specialization of industry, making each community dependent on other communities for the sale of its commodities

and for the satisfaction of its own needs. In place of each family constituting an economic group, there is the greatest division and sub-division of labor among individuals and groups of individuals within the same community. In the face of this profound change from independence to interdependence in the every-day life of the people, it is not a matter of surprise that there should exist a tendency towards a corresponding condition in political affairs. The centralizing measures that have been studied in this essay may be considered as simply applications of the principle of the division of labor to the work of administration; and in this field no less than in the industrial world this principle secures larger and better results with less labor than the system of independent individual and local action.

The effects of these economic and social forces have, naturally, not been confined to the field of governmental administration. On all sides the individualistic and local are being replaced by larger organizations which permit further specialization of functions, co-operation of individual effort, and greater efficiency in results. One needs only to mention railroad consolidations and traffic associations, trusts, boards of trade, manufacturers' associations and trades unions to show the movement in the industrial world; and the same movement can be seen in churches and in scientific, charitable and intellectual societies. Some of these voluntary associations extend beyond political boundaries and present examples of international organizations. In all of these organizations provision is made for some degree of central direction or supervision over the local body or individual member, and in many the concentration of authority has been carried far.

A general movement always tends to carry forward particular factors by its own larger momentum, and undoubtedly this general movement has strengthened the other forces which have brought about centralization in State administration. On the other hand there has been the counteracting force of the earlier theory of local self-government, which has opposed every step towards centralization. In fact, on account of this opposition, State administration is even now much less centralized than other forms of human activity, and it may be suggested that a fuller appreciation of present conditions would open the way to further advances.

A closer study of the general movement toward centralization would bring out with more emphasis what has already been seen in our study of administration in New York, that there are all shades and degrees of centralization. There is as great a contrast between the central authority of the National Wool Manufacturers' Association and of the American Sugar Refining Company as there is between the original authority of the New York State Board of Charities and the present powers of the Commission in Lunacy. Between the extremes are all grades of intermediate positions in the relative authority of local and central bodies. In fact the problem of organization in all spheres of activity is no longer whether there shall be a central authority to co-ordinate and unify the work to be done, but what shall be the nature of the powers of these central bodies, and how large a degree of autonomy may be left to the local institutions. From existing conditions we may expect that the final answer to the problem will not prescribe one form, even within any one department of activity, but that different shades of authority will be found best in different circumstances.

In the particular problem with which we have to deal— that of administrative organization—there are two questions to be determined: (1) The distribution of work between central and local government; what functions may be completely centralized, and what should be assigned to local organs: (2) The reasons for supervision of local authorities by the central government, and the forms and methods of supervision.

In reference to the first point, it may safely be said that those matters in which the interests of the whole country or State are vitally concerned, and those in which the advantages of system and uniformity are overwhelming should be managed by the central government through its own officials. Many of the important interests included in these terms (foreign relations, the army and navy, the postal system, the regulation of the currency, and foreign commerce) are in this country administered by the centralized system of the national government. But the extent of direct State administration in New York is also considerable. General interest has brought this about without question in the management of canals, the control over railroads, insurance and banking companies, the work of factory inspection and the arbitration of labor disputes. The advantages of uniformity and system have led to complete centralization in the care of the insane and in the management of prisons and normal schools. Either or both principles would justify other lines of direct State administration. For example, a force of State police, such as exists in Massachusetts[1] and has been proposed in Pennsylvania, would be of use in suppressing riotous outbreaks too large for the local police without calling on the militia. It is not, however, my purpose to advocate here any extended development along particular lines; but only to indicate the general principles which should direct the establishment of organs of direct State administration.

On the other hand, the functions which should devolve upon local officials, are first of all those matters in which purely local interests are alone concerned, the more distinct

---

[1] R. H. Whitten, *Public Administration in Massachusetts*, pp. 87, 91.

the separation of local interests, the more clear being the
case for local management. But there are also many matters of larger interest which can be attended to better, more
cheaply or more conveniently by local authorities; while
the educational value of political training through local institutions is of much importance in a government whose
basis is popular sovereignty. For these reasons, it is desirable that, in all matters where local knowledge is important,
where the co-operation of private and governmental agencies
can be secured, or where the need of uniformity and rigid
system is less pressing, the detailed administration should be
conferred on a local governing body. It is in accordance
with these principles that local authorities have been assigned powers not merely over works of local improvement
and convenience, but also in matters of general interest, as
poor relief and public education.

It is, however, because these matters of general interest
have been entrusted to local organs, that a central control of
local administration is necessary, and a carefully adjusted co-
operation of local and central organs becomes important.
Since the justification of central control is based on the
principle of general interest, it is necessary to understand
what functions of local administration have this larger public
character. Such matters as the paving, lighting and cleaning of city streets, the prevention of fires, the operation of the
water supply and sewerage systems, are ordinarily of little
consequence to any but the inhabitants of the city. The
State at large is interested only in the same way as it is interested in the private well-being of its individual citizens;
and any large amount of central control over these matters
can be justified only on principles which would go far to
justify an intensive State control of all kinds of individual
and corporate effort

But, even in the large cities, matters of this kind are only a part of the work of local officials; and in their other functions, although the local interest or local knowledge which justifies local administration is well known, the general interest which demands central control is not so often recognized. The sanitary condition of a particular district is of most immediate concern to the inhabitants of the locality; but it it also a matter of serious concern to the surrounding districts, and if conditions likely to cause the diffusion of epidemic diseases are not removed, the danger is one to the entire State, and indeed sometimes to a much larger area. The need for a central authority to supervise the local officials, with power in case of default to take direct action, is almost imperative in such matters.

The interest of the larger communities in questions of poor relief is affected in large measure by the extent of pauperism. The magnitude of the problem in England makes necessary a high degree of centralization to prevent waste and injudicious administration. In this country, however, after deducting those classes which are cared for in State and private institutions, the amount of pauperism to be relieved by local authorities is comparatively small. But even here there is need for some central supervision. Active local interest in public poor relief is generally directed toward maintaining a low poor rate; and to ensure an efficient system affording at least a certain minimum of relief requires some control by higher authorities, who can make comparisons of conditions and results in a large number of localities.

The same principle of ensuring a certain minimum of action on the part of local authorities is the basis of State control over elementary education. In any community having a democratic franchise, the interests of the central government in an intelligent electorate clearly entitle the State to direct the school system so that what it considers a suitable education to secure this result is provided. For higher education, the *a priori* reasons for State control are, perhaps, not so conclusive; but the practical advantages of the Regents' system of academic examinations have established the wisdom of the State supervision.

The prevention and punishment of crime are also matters of more than local interest. It is of great importance to the whole community that no part become a nest of law-breakers or a focus of demoralization through the laxness of police and judicial administration. Even if, in general, laws against crime are enforced, there is a danger where the police are subject to no central control, that particular State laws which are locally unpopular will not be enforced in such localities. This has been particularly the case with laws restricting the sale of liquor; and where State prohibition has been enacted it is only by means of a centralized State police that any degree of enforcement can be secured in some localities. Even where measures rousing such extreme local opposition are considered inadvisable, central control may be called for. The frequent necessity for a co-operation of the police authorities of different cities is of itself an argument for an official organization to make such co-operative action more effective. In reference to jails, it may be pointed out that in the absence of central supervision there is a danger through different conditions in different localities of introducing an arbitrary inequality in the application of punishments.

No argument would seem to be necessary to justify State control over the officials engaged in the assessment and collection of the State revenues. It is beyond question a matter of vital interest to the State government to secure the equitable and efficient enforcement of the State tax laws. Over taxation and expenditure for local purposes the importance of a central control will not, perhaps, be at first admitted.

Yet the need of some control has already been recognized in the constitutional limitations on the debt which may be incurred by a local government, and in the limitations on the power of taxation. An administrative control over such subjects would have the advantage of being more flexible; instead of a fixed and rigid rule, decisions could be adapted to the merits of each case. A central audit of local expenditure, on the same lines as the control over the finances of private corporations for the benefit of their stockholders, would secure are liable publicity in a form which would make possible comparisons with similar results elsewhere.

The central control thus justified by the public interests involved in these various fields of local administration will be in part exercised by the legislature. It can and does enact general provisions of law requiring the local authorities to act in certain ways and limiting their powers and authority. It also enacts a vast amount of special legislation, altering these general provisions in particular cases; but, owing to the large number of such local measures, the great majority of them are passed without any adequate consideration. Other directions in which central control is necessary are manifestly beyond the sphere of legislative action and require a central administrative authority.

Such a central organ can be justified if it does no more than collect information from the different localities, so that the experience of one may be of use to the others. " Power may be localized, but knowledge to be most useful must be centralized; there must be somewhere a focus at which all its scattered rays are collected, that the broken and colored lights which exist elsewhere may find there what is necessary to complete and purify them." [1] What may be accomplished by a central authority with no more than this limited com-

---

[1] J. S. Mill: *Representative Government*, p. 304.

petence has been fully illustrated in the consideration of the work done by the State Board of Charities and the State Board of Health. By keeping themselves in communication with the local officials, collecting information by reports and local investigations, giving advice freely when asked and volunteering it where necessary, these boards have demonstrated their usefulness beyond any doubt.

The work of such advisory boards in making clear the need for a more effective control over local authorities is no less important; and, as we have seen, they have been able to secure further authority in the direction desired. Examples of almost every possible form of central control are to be found in the various kinds of authority now possessed by the New York bureaus of central supervision.[1] The necessity for securing central approval for certain acts of local authorities is one way in which the State Board of Health exercises its powers of control. Conditional grants of state aid are made to both elementary and secondary schools. The power to make rules and regulations for local authorities is possessed by the Superintendent of Public Instruction, the State Board of Charities, and the State Board of Health. Systematic inspections are made by the Boards of Charities and Prisons and the Tax Commissioners. A central audit is made by the agents of the Comptroller and Excise Commissioner. The power to decide appeals from acts of local authorities is held by the State Superintendent of Public Instruction. Even the authority directly to administer local affairs in case of neglect by the local officials is possessed by the State Board of Health.

It will be seen that these various methods of administrative control are primarily for the purpose of inciting the local authorities to action, and only in minor instances to restrain

---

[1] For classification of methods of central control, see: M. R. Maltbie, *English Local Government of To-day*, p. 260; in this *Series*, vol. ix, no. i.

action.   For the latter purpose the judicial control of the
courts, formed in the main to protect private rights, is generally sufficient.   But where local officials are inactive or inefficient, no individual's rights may be seriously and immediately affected, and it is for such matters, where both judicial
and legislative control are unavailable or inadequate, that
administrative control is effective, and hence advisable.

How far the different methods of administrative control
should be made use of in the various fields of governmental
action is a matter of detailed application of general principles,
on which no general rules can be laid down.   The question
has been considered to some extent in the several chapters
on special subjects; but the answer is different not only
for different fields of action, but also for different States
and countries, and in the same country it will change
from time to time as local conditions change.   The stage of
economic and social development in each country must be
taken into consideration, and the practical statesman must
also consider how far it is safe to bring forward plans which,
however well adapted to economic and social conditions,
nevertheless run counter to accepted theories of political
action.

There is, however, one form of administrative action thus
far but slightly used, which could with advantage be much
more generally applied in this State.   The difficulties in the
way of a proper consideration of special legislation could be
removed by making broader general grants of power, and at
the same time requiring the local authorities, before acting
on these powers, to secure the approval of the appropriate
central organ.   This method is now followed in the case of
village construction of sewerage systems on the approval of
the State Board of Health; and the beneficial effects of the
new system have been noted.   The authority of the Regents
to grant charters of incorporation to educational institu-

tions is another example of the same method. A general application of this method would secure the advantages of special acts for special local conditions with a more careful consideration of the local conditions by a competent authority. The action of the legislature on local bills is purely formal, and the question is simply one of substituting for a committee sitting for only a few months, and whose members are also engaged in other duties, a more permanent authority, continuously on duty and devoting its attention exclusively to one class of measures. The formal action of the legislature could be retained, as in England, where the Provisional Orders of the Local Government Board are confirmed by Act of Parliament at the following session.

The central authorities of administrative control in New York State show three distinct types of organization: in some instances there is a single commissioner or superintendent, with a fairly large salary; in others there is a board of three commissioners receiving more moderate salaries; and in still others there is a large board of commissioners receiving a trifling compensation, giving only a part of their time to the work, but with one or more salaried executive officers who are constantly on duty. This variation suggests some consideration of the relative advantages of the different forms of organization of the central authority.

When the central administrative control is but small and mainly of an advisory nature, the large board form of organization offers several advantages. On such boards men of large experience and broad intelligence will accept positions for the opportunity to perform a service which in most cases has a humanitarian aspect. In introducing a system of central control, such commissioners are able to exercise a more potent influence by means of occasional visits and wise suggestions than could be accomplished by a more systematic visitation by inspectors with larger powers whose visits were accompanied by the issue of orders and the exercise of compulsory powers.

When, however, it is deemed best to apply a more authoritative control, and a large force of subordinate inspectors or agents are employed, these can be much better directed by a single head than by a board. At the same time, with this more continuous inspection and more authoritative control, the need for the especial service which the unsalaried commissioners perform becomes less pressing. The Regents of the University, however, show the possibility of combining the two systems by retaining the board as an authority of general direction over the executive officer who controls the details of the work.

The intermediate form seems to have little to justify it as an authority to supervise local officials. The moderate salary which accompanies the triplication of the positions ensures the selection of men of moderate abilities, since the positions have no such honorary dignity as those on the large unpaid boards. At the same time the number of commissioners is too small to make possible any effective investigation of local conditions. There are no subordinate agents, and if there were such, they could be better directed by a single head. This form has advantages in such a case as the Commission in Lunacy, whose control is over a comparatively small number of state institutions; but as an authority to supervise local officials over the entire state it seems in every way inferior to both of the other types.

Another problem of organization which presents itself is the co-ordination of the many scattered and heterogeneous central authorities. The task indeed involves the entire list of State administrative bureaus; but even in those which have been considered in this essay the possibility of advantageous union is evident. Here again, consolidation does not mean the abolition of existing organs; but rather their organization as bureaus in a co-ordinated system of State departments, so as to secure the advantages of concentration of knowledge and co-operation in action. The union of the two state educational bureaus has already been discussed. Similarly the State Comptroller, the Excise Commissioner and the Tax Commissioners might be united under a Secretary of the Treasury, following the precedent of the national government. Other combinations, of the different bureaus which have not come within the scope of this essay, are also possible and advisable. If the forty independent state bureaus could be thus brought into a related administrative system under a few department secretaries, not only would there be increased efficiency in the working of the state administration, but it would make possible an explanation of the system that would create a popular understanding of what the State government is and does.